The Business
of
ORGANIZED CRIME

The Business
of
ORGANIZED CRIME
A Cosa Nostra Family

Annelise Graebner Anderson

Hoover Institution Press
Stanford University, Stanford, California

Hoover Institution Publication 201

© 1979 by the Board of Trustees of the
  Leland Stanford Junior University
All rights reserved
International Standard Book Number: 0−8179−7011−8
Library of Congress Catalog Card Number: 78−59464
Printed in the United States of America
Second Printing, 1980

For my mother and father

CONTENTS

ACKNOWLEDGMENTS

I would like to thank Professors James Kuhn, Eli Ginzberg, Ivar Berg, and David Lewin, all of Columbia University, for their advice and encouragement on this study.

A great many people in the law enforcement community and elsewhere also gave generously of their time and energies in discussing ideas and otherwise assisting me. I wish to thank especially Martin Danziger and Gerald Shur, both at the time attorneys with the U.S. Department of Justice.

Many other people provided significant encouragement for this project or read various drafts of the manuscript and offered helpful suggestions. They include Martin Anderson, Harry Bratt, Donald Cressey, Bryce Harlow, John Kaplan, Francis Ianni, Thomas Moore, Henry Ruth, Thomas C. Schelling, and William Vickrey.

Lois Strand did a superb job of typing the manuscript, and Meryl Lanning of editing. Mickey Hamilton of the Hoover Institution Press managed the publishing process with efficiency and competence.

Early stages of the research were financed by a grant from the National Institute of Law Enforcement and Criminal Justice of the Law Enforcement Assistance Administration, U.S. Department of Justice, where I was a visiting fellow for a year. Far more important to me than the funds was the association with others concerned about organized crime and knowledgeable about the criminal justice system in the United States.

ANNELISE GRAEBNER ANDERSON

INTRODUCTION

In the early days of Prohibition, a group of young men of Italian national origin formed a gang to supply alcoholic beverages to the thirsty population of one of the largest cities in the United States. By 1970, one of these young men had become the head of a Mafia family in what was still one of the nation's twenty largest cities. He and his associates from Prohibition days, and the members they had since recruited into their group, were now in illegal gambling and loan-sharking and owned a considerable number of legitimate businesses. They went about their business, were generally able to "fix" their problems with the local criminal justice system, were hawkish on Vietnam, opposed the counter-culture, contributed to political candidates of both parties, boasted when their children were accepted at college, and worried about recruiting new members and being called to testify before grand juries. I call them the Benguerra family, and this book is a case study of the group, their illegal market activities, and their legitimate business interests.*

In undertaking the research for this study, I was initially interested in the reasons why organized criminal groups own and operate legitimate businesses and undertake other legitimate savings and investment. Is legitimate business investment an aggressive effort to obtain extraordinary profits through illegal methods, or is it an effort to become respectable and assume accepted roles in American life? Neither view was confirmed. As the study progressed, I realized that to understand the legitimate business involvements of members of the group, I would

---

*Benguerra, the surname of the boss of the family, is a pseudonym. It was constructed from the letters of my maiden name, Graebner, with a *u* added for phonetic reasons.

need to understand their illegal market enterprises and opportunities and the problems they encounter as operators of illegal market enterprises. It became apparent that organized illegal market activity generates a need for legitimate business ownership and affects the economic benefits to be gained from particular types of legitimate business investment.

It also became apparent that the nature of the group itself is important. Some writers explicitly or implicitly view an organized criminal group as a business firm, but the Benguerra family does not function as a business firm. It does have the hierarchical organization structure described by many writers as typical of Italian organized criminal groups—a boss, an underboss, a counselor to the boss, and captains or heads of groups; below this administrative hierarchy are the ordinary members. The leaders of the group perform what are essentially quasi-governmental functions—they make rules, adjudicate disputes, and enforce decisions over a variety of matters—but the boss is not the chief executive officer of a business empire. Instead, members of the group have formed several firms, often partnerships, that operate in illegal markets. The organization of these illegal enterprises is not one-to-one with the group's governing structure. The businesses are owned by individual members rather than the group, although in numbers gambling the group does function as a cartel, controlling entry and probably also prices.

The situation is the same in legitimate business. Individuals rather than the group make decisions about entry into legitimate business and may enter alone, in partnership with other members of the group, or in partnership with nonmembers.

A group rather than a particular illegal market or a selection of examples of organized criminal activity was chosen for study because organized criminal groups with defined membership do exist, and they have been a major force in certain fields of illegal market activity in the United States in the last several decades. Second, many of the views or hypotheses about organized crime presented in the literature concern groups rather than illegal market enterprises—for example, the hypotheses that organized criminal groups are (implicitly) business firms functioning as formal organizations, or that certain core markets provide the foundation for the existence of organized criminal groups.

The various hypotheses offered in the literature are presented in the terminology of more than one academic discipline and are somewhat imprecise and diverse. Whatever its diversity, however, the literature on organized crime is concerned with organized criminal *groups*. Ianni's study of kinship, for example, is explicit in selecting a group (or rather the top-level members of a group) as the unit of study. In studying loansharking, Seidl found it necessary to distinguish between loanshark organizations and the criminal organizations (here called groups) of which they were a part.[1]

Organized crime as a matter of concern in the United States, and thus as a public policy problem, is also centered around the organized criminal group rather than specific illegal markets. The assumption is that an organized criminal group is more dangerous than isolated illegal enterprises because it can do many things that less well organized criminal enterprises may fail to do: corrupt public officials, use violence or the threat of violence effectively, and expand into areas that would not otherwise be controlled or influenced by large criminal organizations, including legitimate business.

The Benguerra family was selected for study because it is a major organized criminal group with reasonably self-contained operations, about which more and better information was available than about other groups. This group has 75 members, all men of Italian national origin. In addition, the group has sixteen close associates: men who work closely with at least two members of the group, know a good deal about the illegal activities in which members engage, and qualify for possible membership in that they are also Italian-Americans. Not all the members of the group are engaged in illegal activity; not all are wealthy; and half of them are over 60 years of age. The primary illegal market activities of the group are numbers lotteries and loansharking. Two other lesser organized criminal groups of other minority ethnic backgrounds operate in the same city.

To call the group typical of Italian organized criminal groups in the United States would be too strong. Nevertheless, many such groups share the characteristics of size, illegal market activity, and coexistence with other organized criminal groups in the same city.

The Benguerra family is one of the 24 groups identified as the "core" of organized crime in the United States by the task force on organized crime of the President's Commission on Law Enforcement and Administration of Justice.[2] An Italian group was selected for study because organized crime in this country has been dominated by Italian organized criminal groups since the 1930s. Although this dominance may be

exaggerated in the public mind and in the views of law enforcement officials, to ignore it and the success of these groups would be to ignore an
important matter. This dominance of Italian organized crime—partly
real and partly assumed—also means that more comprehensive data are
available on these groups than on groups formed by others.

The data sources for this study were provided by a federal agency and
supplemented by public documents and interviews with people in the
law enforcement community. The agency made two requests: that it not
be identified, except as a federal agency, and that the city in which the
Benguerra family operates not be identified. The agency was also concerned with the possibility that informants could be identified but was
reassured, after reading a draft of the manuscript, by the aggregate use
made of the data. Although I could probably have persuaded them to
allow me to identify the city, not identifying it allows a more detailed
presentation of data about the group.

Although the information in the data sources was less detailed than
would be desirable for a study of this type, it is likely to be as comprehensive as any compilation of information about an organized criminal
group. The Appendix discusses the kinds of information available in the
data sources and how it was handled. In general, information about the
group was available for 1960 to 1970. The years 1968–1969 were
chosen for in-depth analysis, and the description of the illegal enterprises and legitimate investments of the group, insofar as it concerns a
point in time, is a description as of January 1, 1970.

The study concentrates on the illegal market activities and legitimate
business investments of group members and close associates, rather than
on the interaction between organized criminal activity and law enforcement. This emphasis is intentional. A great deal more is known about
law enforcement against organized crime than about organized crime
itself. There are no published statistics on organized crime comparable,
for example, to statistics on burglaries known to the police or the value
of goods stolen. Nor are there systematic statistics on illegal gambling[3]
and loansharking, related corruption of public officials, or the use of
violence. With the exception of this study, there is, to my knowledge, no
systematic survey of the legitimate business activities of the members and
associates of an organized criminal group that relates legitimate investment to the illegal market enterprises that are the primarily illegal
activity of the members.

Concern about organized crime increased during the 1960s. In 1967 the government's task force report on organized crime, mentioned above, was published. Two years later two excellent overviews of organized crime appeared, one by sociologist Donald Cressey and the other by ex–New York City policeman Ralph Salerno.[4] Again, new legislation, much of it recommended by the task force report, was passed, and both federal and state efforts to combat organized crime were increased.

But organized crime continues to generate both headlines and public concern. Unfortunately, data are not available for an empirical study of the effectiveness of the new legislation passed or the greatly increased resources allocated to combat organized crime since the early 1960s.

This study was undertaken in the belief that, to advance our knowledge of organized crime and eventually reach a point where we can compare organized crime "rates" at different points in time or in different localities, and thereby evaluate the effect of alternative public policies in terms of their benefits in reducing the damages done by organized crime, research more focused and detailed is necessary. To go beyond the general overview, research can focus on illegal markets for goods and services, in which from time to time organized criminal groups may be active or controlling, or it can focus on specific organized criminal groups. John Seidl and Louis Gasper chose the first approach, studying loansharking and illegal traffic in cigarettes, respectively;[5] and of course numerous studies of illegal drug markets have been made. Ianni chose the latter approach, using a participant-observer method to gather data on the top members of an organized criminal group. This book also takes the latter approach: it is an in-depth study of an organized criminal group—in this instance, all the members of the group, unsuccessful as well as successful, and both their illegal and legitimate activities and the interaction between them.

Unlike Ianni's study, based on a participant-observer field method, my work is based primarily on data provided by a federal law enforcement agency. Each approach has its strengths and its weaknesses. The participant-observer is likely to obtain less information—or be less free to use it—about illegal activity and may influence the behavior of the group he or she attempts to observe. Investigative agency data, on the other hand, has been collected for purposes other than social science research, lacks many items of information that would be easy to observe and record but are not recorded because they are not valuable in law enforcement, and takes the researcher one step away from the actual participants.

Nevertheless, federal agencies have been collecting data more or less systematically over a long period of time, and similar kinds of information are collected by state and sometimes local agencies by what are often called organized crime intelligence units. A study based on data of investigative agencies can thus be replicated at another time or another locale, whereas the participant-observer study probably cannot.

Given an interest, investigative agencies could begin to collect more systematically data with social science relevance, so that they could make periodic reports of the state of organized crime in a city: the volume of illegal market transactions, the number of violent acts associated with organized criminal activity, the kinds, size, and number of legitimate businesses owned by members and associates of different groups, the extent to which patterns of control of lines of trade or labor unions can be observed, and even perhaps the extent of corruption of public officials. With such periodic studies, it should be possible to compare the operation of organized criminal groups in different places to determine, for example, why one group is more violent than another; why one group's activities in legitimate business are extortionate or characterized by the use of criminal means to attempt to monopolize, whereas another's are not; or why the organization of an illegal market such as gambling or loansharking, the prices charged for the illegal goods or services, and the fairness and honesty toward consumers differ in different cities.

The ultimate goal, of course, is to be able to relate alternative public policies and practices with respect to law enforcement against organized crime to their costs and their benefits in controlling and reducing the harm done by organized crime. This goal is different from that of law enforcement officials, who offer as criteria of success the numbers of indictments and convictions they achieve. Public policy concerning crime necessarily, however, involves government in its most fundamental characteristic—the legitimatized power to use force within the area of its jurisdiction to take property and restrict freedom—in the modern state, in accordance with enacted statute.[6] The use of such powers involves costs in privacy and freedom, and costs of potential misuse of governmental powers currently and in the future. With more legislation and more money, investigators and prosecutors should of course be able to increase indictments and convictions. This does not tell us, however, whether the world would be a better place to live as a result, or whether the new legislation would be worth the resources devoted to it or the decrease in freedom or privacy that may accompany it.

The kinds of data on which this study is based are available in the files of agencies that investigate organized criminal activity. This type of case study could thus be done on organized criminal groups in other cities, and it could be repeated in the same city to determine changes over time. If this were done, we could begin to get some idea of the scope of the problem of organized crime; of whether the problem is increasing, decreasing, or changing; and of the effectiveness of alternative legislation and enforcement activities in combatting the problem.

I

THE MAFIA:
CONTROVERSY AND EVIDENCE

While the Benguerra family has gone about its business, the American public has followed its exploits and those of other organized criminal groups through anecdotal and often inflammatory newspaper accounts. In 1951 Senator Estes Kefauver's Special Committee to Investigate Organized Crime in Interstate Commerce held televised hearings; the Senator declared that a nationwide crime syndicate existed in the United States, and the Committee's report identified that syndicate as the Mafia.[1] Edward G. Robinson, James Cagney, and others made movies in which they played gangsters, and on television Ephraim Zimbalist, Jr., fought the Mafia, or the Syndicate, for the FBI and the American people. *Life* reported on gangsters from all over the country attending a meeting—or a barbeque—in Apalachin, New York, in 1957.[2] Organized crime in the 1950s seemed to be a thriving industry, for the gangsters, for congressmen, for the police, prosecutors, and lawyers, and for the media. The public was at least entertained.

The idea of a nationwide crime syndicate had its critics. In an article first published in 1953, Daniel Bell, a Columbia University sociologist, described urban rackets—"illicit activity organized for continuing profit, rather than individual illegal acts"—as "one of the queer ladders of social mobility in American life." But he opposed the Kefauver Committee's description of the Mafia as a nationwide crime syndicate: "Unfortunately for a good story—and the existence of the Mafia would be a whale of a story—neither the Senate Crime Committee in its testimony, nor Kefauver in his book, presented any real evidence that the Mafia exists as a functioning organization."[3]

Life's report of the meeting in Apalachin, attended by perhaps 60 or more organized crime figures, increased public concern. During the 1960s new laws were passed, more money was appropriated by Congress for the fight against organized crime, and interagency groups—called strike forces—were set up under the auspices of the Organized Crime and Racketeering Section of the U.S. Department of Justice to investigate and prosecute organized crime in selected cities.

In 1963 and 1964 Joseph Valachi testified before a U.S. Senate committee investigating narcotics traffic. Valachi claimed to be a member of an organized criminal group called a family. According to him the various groups in the United States supposedly make up something called *Cosa Nostra* (our thing), or what Kefauver had called the *Mafia*—a term Valachi claimed he had never heard used.[4]

In 1966, the Oyster Bay conferences on organized crime brought together over 40 experienced representatives of law enforcement agencies, prosecutive agencies, and crime commissions and produced the following statement about organized crime:

> Organized crime is the product of a self-perpetuating conspiracy to wring exorbitant profits from our society by any means—fair and foul, legal and illegal. Despite personnel changes, the conspiratorial entity continues. It is a malignant parasite which fattens on human weakness. It survives on fear and corruption. By one or another means, it obtains a high degree of immunity from the law.
>
> It is totalitarian in its organization. A way of life, it imposes rigid discipline on underlings who do the dirty work while the top men of organized crime are generally insulated from the criminal act and the consequent danger of prosecution.[5]

The task force on organized crime of the President's Commission on Law Enforcement and Administration of Justice, reporting in 1967, had this to say:

> Organized crime is a society that seeks to operate outside the control of the American people and their government. It involves thousands of criminals, working within structures as complex as those of any large corporation, subject to laws more rigidly enforced than those of legitimate governments. Its actions are not impulsive but rather the result of intricate conspiracies, carried on over many years and aimed at gaining control over whole fields of activity in order to amass huge profits.
>
> The core of organized crime activity is the supplying of illegal goods and services—gambling, loan sharking, narcotics, and other forms of vice—to countless numbers of citizen customers. But organized crime is

also extensively and deeply involved in legitimate business and in labor unions. Here it employs illegitimate methods—monopolization, terrorism, extortion, tax evasion—to drive out or control lawful ownership and leadership and to exact illegal profits from the public. And to carry on its many activities secure from governmental interference, organized crime corrupts public officials.

The task force, using data provided by the Department of Justice, found the Italian-American groups central to organized crime:

> Today the core of organized crime in the United States consists of 24 groups operating as criminal cartels in large cities across the Nation. Their membership is exclusively men of Italian descent, they are in frequent communication with each other, and their smooth functioning is insured by a national body of overseers.[6]

In spite of conflict with non-Italian criminal groups, competition among groups, and internal dissension leading to a variety of realignments, as organizations these groups have a record of survival and continuity going back to the 1930s. The origins of many of them can be traced to the days of Prohibition and before.[7]

The task force report was followed in 1969 by two excellent overviews of organized crime, both by men who had been consultants to the task force. In *Theft of the Nation,* sociologist Donald Cressey emphasized the centrality of Italian organized criminal groups and their nature as formal organizations:

> I [believe] that the Cosa Nostra organization is so extensive, so powerful, and so central that precise description and control of it would be description of all but a tiny part of all organized crime . . . we do know enough about the structure of Cosa Nostra to conclude that it is indeed an organization with both formal and informal aspects. . . . Cosa Nostra exists independently of its current personnel, as does any big business or government. Business, government, and Cosa Nostra go on despite complete turnover in the personnel occupying the various positions making up the organization. . . . No man is indispensable. Organization, or "structure," not persons, gives Cosa Nostra its self-perpetuating character.

Cressey goes on to describe the structure of the families that make up Cosa Nostra: each has a boss, an underboss, a counselor to the boss (a staff rather than a line position), captains (or heads of smaller groups), and ordinary members—soldiers. "The highest ruling body in Cosa Nostra is the 'Commission'. . . . The Commission is made up of the rulers of the most powerful 'families,' which are located in large cities."[8]

Ralph Salerno, formerly with the Central Intelligence Bureau of the New York City Police Department, provides in *The Crime Confederation* essentially the same description as Cressey's:

> . . . the fact is that the Italian gangs—Cosa Nostra—do make up the center of organized crime: a group of 5000 to 7500 formal members to which an equal number of non-Italian group members are linked by alliances and for which independent groups and individual criminals work. . . . The Boss of the Cosa Nostra family schematized above may or may not sit on the Commission, which is what Cosa Nostra calls its national council."[9]

It was also in 1969 that Gordon Hawkins, taking Daniel Bell one step further, published an article declaring that the Mafia had the same status as God: you might believe, but proof is hard to come by. Hawkins appropriately attacks statements of politicians, law enforcement officials, and others comparable to those presented in the task force report of the President's Commission and the report of the Oyster Bay conferences quoted earlier, with reference to both the existence of the organization, its structure, and its code of conduct for members. He reviews Cressey's contribution to the task force report, noting that "the details of criminal hierarchies given by Professor Cressey and others in the literature on organized crime are curiously reminiscent of the details of celestial hierarchies to be found in the literature of angelology."[10]

Hawkins, like Bell, acknowledges the existence of racketeering and accepts Harvard economist Thomas C. Schelling's description of "large-scale continuing firms with the internal organization of a large enterprise, and with a conscious effort to control the market."[11] But according to Hawkins, the question is "whether in addition to such 'large-scale continuing firms' located in various parts of the country, there is a national syndicate that dominates organized crime throughout the country—one large nationwide criminal organization that controls the majority, if not all, of the local undertakings."[12] He concludes that there is no evidence to support this hypothesis. His arguments are essentially based on what he considers to be internal contradictions in Joseph Valachi's testimony before a Senate committee in 1963 and 1964 and on lack of corroboration of that testimony.

The question Hawkins has set up—whether a national syndicate controls organized crime throughout the country, even on the local level— is really a straw man. Politicians and law enforcement officials can be expected to make extreme and unqualified statements about the extent and dangers of organized crime: it gives them visibility, it develops public support for an increase in the law enforcement budget, it may discourage the citizenry from purchasing illegal goods and services. Apprehension and prosecution of people engaged in organized criminal activity can be sufficiently attention-getting to propel a prosecutor into elective office, as Thomas Dewey demonstrated. But academia could be fully occupied rebutting the unqualified statements of politicians if it took this as its assigned task.

The real question is not whether the Mafia exists, as if the answer were, for all time, yes or no. The real question is how crime in the United States is organized, if at all. What kinds of organizations exist? Are there criminal organizations that recognize members and nonmembers? Are they formal organizations in some sense of that term? What kind of survival capability do they have, and why? How did they develop, and in what kinds of crime are they involved? In what illegal markets do they operate, what makes these markets attractive, and why have the markets in which they are involved changed over time? Are there any groups made up of single ethnic minorities? If so, why—and if so, are groups of a particular ethnic minority in touch with one another? To what extent do they cooperate with each other, and with groups of other ethnic minorities? How is the picture changing over time? If a number of organizations whose members are of a single ethnic minority (say, Italian) can be identified, how important is this particular group of organizations in the totality of what we might define—with some difficulty—as "organized crime"?

In 1972 Francis A. J. Ianni, a cultural anthropologist, published a study of a New York City Italian-American organized crime family. He, like Hawkins, devotes some space to objections to straw-man statements about organized crime. In contrast to Cressey, he presents the view that organized criminal groups of Italian descent are not formal organizations, consciously structured to achieve a specific set of goals:

> Rather, they are traditional social systems, products of culture, and responsive to cultural change. Far from being hierarchies of organizational positions, which can be diagrammed and then changed by recasting the organization chart, they are patterns of relationships among individuals, which have the force of kinship, and which can be changed only by drastic, often fatal, action.[13]

While Ianni rejects any national conspiracy theory, he does acknowledge the existence of Italian-American crime syndicates and notes the extensive intermarriage among them and the fact that virtually every

Italian-American identified as involved in organized crime is of southern
Italian peasant origin, usually Sicilian. The crime families are, he concludes, lineages linked together into a composite clan:

> We believe it is the universality of this clan organization and the strength
> of its shared behavior system which makes Italian-American criminal syn-
> dicates seem so similar. And we believe that it is this similarity which has
> inclined observers to maintain that the different crime families consti-
> tute some sort of highly organized national or even international crime
> conspiracy.[14]

Given the range of opinion, from Kefauver to Hawkins and from
Cressey to Ianni, on the existence of organized criminal groups and a
national crime syndicate, whether or not Italian-American organized
criminal groups are formal organizations, and the like, the reader would
perhaps appreciate the opportunity to make an independent judgment
on the basis of primary sources. In 1969, soon after Hawkins' article was
published, the Federal District Court in Newark, New Jersey, made
public as part of court cases documents based on electronic surveillance
by the Federal Bureau of Investigation (FBI) of two Italian organized
crime figures covering a period of many months in the early 1960s.
These documents include many verbatim transcripts of conversations
among members of organized criminal groups. The transcripts, along
with published sections of other transcripts of conversations overheard
on other wiretaps, are perhaps the only truly primary source documents
on organized crime that exist. Some argument could be made for
including public testimony or writings of organized crime figures in this
category, but such sources are open to suspicion because of the relationship of those who testify with law enforcement officials.

One of these documents, that dealing with Samuel Rizzo de Cavalcante of New Jersey, covers the period from May 7, 1964, to July 12,
1965, with some material from 1962. The document is known as the de
Cavalcante Transcripts because it is based primarily on transcripts of
conversations in which de Cavalcante is a participant. The conversations
were overheard by four microphones; one of the mikes was in his office.
Over 2,000 pages long, the de Cavalcante Transcripts are actually
internal FBI papers, sometimes providing a log of the content of what
was overheard, sometimes summarizing the material in the form of
memoranda, and, most interesting, sometimes quoting conversations
verbatim. The portions of the document quoted below are entirely from

the verbatim conversations, although some explanatory remarks are offered.

It is tempting to let the reader do the work of arriving at the implied structure of Italian organized crime in the United States as it existed at the time the microphones were in place. This would be asking a great deal, however, because the reader necessarily drops into the middle of conversations based on established relationships among people who share common knowledge. Furthermore, participants use both English and Italian, or Sicilian. The following introduction to the transcripts is offered not as a definitive conclusion, but rather as an hypothesis that explains most of the remarks.

An organized criminal group—a crime syndicate—is called a *borgata,* or family, and operates in a reasonably defined geographical area; there are several, possibly many, such groups in the United States in different cities. These families are membership organizations. When a member refers to his own family, he may call it "our outfit" or "our organization." When an individual becomes a member of the group, he is "made," and this is an identifiable event: members know how long they have been members.

A family is headed by a boss. A boss has a counselor, or *consiglieri.* There is also an underboss; these three positions are the most important. Below the level of underboss are *caporegimes* (*capos,* for short) or captains, who are heads of *regimes.* Sometimes capos are called *capodecinas,* and regimes can be called *decines.* Regimes are made up of soldiers, the lowest ranking members. All members above the level of soldier are part of the administration (the governing structure) of the family.

The Italian-American families as a group are *Cosa Nostra*—our thing. Any member of a family is thus part of Cosa Nostra, and since he is part of "our thing," he is "a friend of ours." This phrase distinguishes members of any family from people who are members of no family, and it is more commonly heard in the Italian than in English: *amica nostra, amico nostro, amico nos*—all alternative spellings that mean friend or friends of ours.*

---

*An Italian or Sicilian language expert could perhaps identify the correct spelling and grammar. The transcripts are based on what the FBI *heard,* and they may have heard incorrectly; also, the speakers do not speak standard English, and there is no reason to assume that they speak standard Italian or Sicilian.

Thus, when de Cavalcante says, "Even if he's not with us, he's still a friend of ours," he presumably means that this person is not a member of the family of which de Cavalcante is boss, but is a member of some other family. A member may ask about someone, "Is he a friend of ours?" If he is, the next question might be, "Who is he with?" which means, what family does he belong to? This is asked in much the same way businessmen say to each other, "Who are you with?" expecting the name of a business firm in reply.

There is a Commission. According to de Cavalcante, the bosses of all the families are supposed to get together every five years and select, from among themselves, the members of the Commission. Bosses not on the Commission may be represented by a boss who is a member. Like any committee, some members are more influential than others, and some members follow the lead of others. On one occasion the participants refer to the members of the Commission as chief justices, by analogy viewing the Commission as their supreme court.

The time period covered by the transcripts quoted here—August 31, 1964 to June 16, 1965—was a time of considerable turmoil. The Commission was in the process of objecting to the behavior of Joseph Bonanno, boss of a New York family and a Commission member; in time they deposed him, and a new boss took his place. Members of the Bonanno family faced the problem of loyalty to him or loyalty to the Commission and those whom the Commission put "in charge" of the family.

All the quotations from the transcripts that follow were overheard from the FBI-placed microphone known as source NK 2461-C*, in de Cavalcante's office at his plumbing and heating business in Kenilworth, New Jersey. The FBI memoranda never mention the microphone; instead, NK 2461-C* "reports" and "advises." In an FBI airtel dated September 24, 1964, to the Director, FBI, from Special Agent in Charge, Newark, the presence of the microphone is referred to obliquely:

> Contact with NK 2461-C* was initiated on 8/31/64 and from that date information was received indicating that Samuel Rizzo de Cavalcante was acting as an intermediary in the dispute between Joseph Bonanno and the Cosa Nostra Commission . . . Verbatim transcripts are being prepared where pertinent . . . Although it appears that de Cavalcante may take no active part in the dispute from now on, it is believed that he will probably be kept informed and in turn will discuss it with his visitors. As can be readily appreciated, NK 2461-C* is an unusually well placed source.

Newark again recommends that any investigative activity which might result in the discontinuance of de Cavalcante's use of his headquarters be avoided if possible.[15]

Memos written in later months often end with the warning, "Information from this source is not to be disseminated outside the Bureau, nor should it be alluded to in any conversations with informants, subjects, or suspects."[16]

Within the quoted materials, the explanations in parentheses have been added by the FBI to translate a foreign or slang term, identify a person by last name, and the like. I have added explanatory material outside the quotations to assist the reader.

In the first conversation, Joseph Bonanno is identified as a member of the Commission and head of a family, or borgata; later, Sam de Cavalcante and Joe Sferra discuss finding jobs for members of Carl Gambino's family.

Conversation # 1
Place: Office of Samuel de Cavalante, Kenilworth, New Jersey
Date: August 31, 1964
Participants: Sam de Cavalcante, Joe Sferra
Source: FBI memorandum to Special Agent in Charge, Newark, from Special Agent John P. Wilcus, September 9, 1964

SFERRA:	So what's new?
DE CAVALCANTE:	Oh—a little trouble over there, in New York.
SFERRA:	New York?
DE CAVALCANTE:	Yeah. Close the door. Nobody's supposed to know.
SFERRA:	Sam, if you don't want to tell me you don't have to tell me.
DE CAVALCANTE:	It's about Joe Bonanno's *borgata* (family). The Commission don't like the way he's comporting himself.
SFERRA:	The way he's conducting himself you mean?
DE CAVALCANTE:	Well, he made his son *consiglieri*—and it's been reported—the son, that he don't show up. They sent for him and he didn't show up. And they want to throw him out of the Commission. I feel sorry for the guy, you know. He's not a bad guy.
SFERRA:	How old is he?

DE CAVALCANTE: Sixty, sixty-two.

[Joe Sferra is Business Agent for Local 394 Hod Carriers and Common Laborers Union, Elizabeth, New Jersey; some men have been laid off a job they were working on.]

DE CAVALCANTE: Joe, over here, even if he's not with us he's still a friend of ours.

SFERRA: Hey Sam—that guy is only home one day. He got laid off Thursday!

DE CAVALCANTE: I know . . . he told me he was laid off. I told him . . .

SFERRA: So what'd he run to you for? Don't I know it? He's got a lot of nerve.

DE CAVALCANTE: Joe, nerve or no nerve, you know I promised Carl Gambino that we'd treat their men better than our own people. And I want it to be that way.

SFERRA: Sam, there are *amica nostra* that belong with us that got laid off of the same job, too.

DE CAVALCANTE: I know that. But I want these people—I don't want that as long as they're *amica nostra* that they have to go to the hall. (Presumably reference is to union hiring hall.) . . . You see, Joe, over here, I'm trying to build a good relationship with everybody in the Commission. Our *borgata* is small but we could do things as good as anybody else. And I told you—as long as they are *amica nostra* I don't want them to go to the hall. I want them to keep working before anybody else.[17]

The second conversation uses the term "made" for obtaining membership status, and shows that one becomes a member of a particular family or outfit.

Conversation #2
Place: The same
Date: October 14, 1964
Participants: Samuel de Cavalcante and Antony Santoli (Jack Panels)
Source: FBI memorandum to Special Agent in Charge, Newark, from Special Agent John P. Wilcus, October 28, 1964

[According to the FBI, de Cavalcante had asked Santoli how long he had waited to be admitted to the organization.]

SANTOLI:	I'll bet I waited 12 years or more.
DE CAVALCANTE:	That right?
SANTOLI:	I worked! I've been—we've been doing favors for the organization 30 years! How long am I made now? Eight years? Ten years?
DE CAVALCANTE:	I've been in 22 years. I've been in as long as Jerry has. I could have been made with Albert's outfit. I could have been made with Joe Bruno.[18]

In the third conversation de Cavalcante discusses the powers of the Commission and the problems in the Bonanno family at length with Joseph Zicarelli, a member of the Bonanno family and a close friend of de Cavalcante's. By implication, one reason why Bonanno did not respond to the Commission's request to see him was his fear of being murdered (hit). Zicarelli seems to consider this one of the risks of membership. The members of the Commission are referred to as chief justices. De Cavalcante finds ample precedent for the Commission to step in and give orders to a family for a period of time. He talks about enforcing right and wrong as a purpose of the Commission. The theme of doing what is right comes up frequently when there is a judicial decision to be made.

Conversation #3
Place: The same
Date: October 21, 1964
Participants: Samuel de Cavalcante, Joseph Arthur Zicarelli (Joe Bayonne)
Source: FBI airtel to Director, FBI, from Special Agent in Charge, Newark, New Jersey, October 25, 1964

DE CAVALCANTE:	Joe, this is strictly between you and I . . . I told Joe the Commission has got nothing against any of you fellows. They respect all your people as friends of ours. But they will not recognize Joe, his son (Salvatore Vincent Bonanno, also known as Bill) and Johnny (Burns—true name John Morales).
ZICARELLI:	(*Incredulously*) Joe, his son, *and* Johnny?
DE CAVALCANTE:	Yeah. Well, when they don't recognize a Boss . . .
ZICARELLI:	Then all three goes.

DE CAVALCANTE: The whole three . . . The Commission is out to hurt no one—not even Joe Bonanno. But they don't want no one else hurt either.

ZICARELLI: Who?

DE CAVALCANTE: Right in your own outfit. When Joe defies the Commission he is defying the whole world.

ZICARELLI: The way I hear the story he's not defying anybody . . .

DE CAVALCANTE: Joe, I pleaded with this man, you know that . . . Now—you see like I told him "You think you're being accused falsely why the hell don't you run over there? Or get on your bicycle and start seeing people? This guy wants to ignore the whole damn thing! He knows it can't be done! The Commission was formed by people—all bosses—who have given the Commission the right to supersede any boss. Joe knows that! He made the rules! Now, the Commission thinks, "Here, this guy's a boss and he's not treating his people right . . ."

[*Sometime later*]

DE CAVALCANTE: Joe—the Commission can come in and say, "Boys, we sent for your boss . . ." Say the Commission calls me and I ignore them . . .

ZICARELLI: Yeah.

DE CAVALCANTE: The Commission has the right to revoke me . . .

ZICARELLI: Well, is he ignoring the messages?

DE CAVALCANTE: Yeah . . . See he made another bad move—he put Gasparino—he's a *caporegime*—they put him on the shelf with the *amico nos* . . .

ZICARELLI: Temporarily!

DE CAVALCANTE: . . . because he didn't come in when he was asked to come in. Now, who is he? He's asked to come in to the Commission and he refuses.

ZICARELLI: But this is within his own family! Why didn't Gasparino come in when all the captains assembled?

DE CAVALCANTE: Well, he probably had his own rights.

ZICARELLI: Where does this make sense, Sam? Where can he have his own rights? . . . He was told! From what I understand, he was given all the extensions in the world, that nobody meant no harm or nothing. There

	was just some misunderstanding and they're holding a meeting. The guy's a captain! What kind of an example is he?
DE CAVALCANTE:	Well . . .
ZICARELLI:	Right or wrong—you go. I guarantee you one thing—this guy here is my boss. Right or wrong if he calls me—I'm going. If I'm gonna get hit—the hell with it. I get hit and that's the end of it. It don't make sense to me!
DE CAVALCANTE:	This guy refuses to go, right?
ZICARELLI:	Yeah.
DE CAVALCANTE:	And he was put on the shelf.
ZICARELLI:	Temporarily.
DE CAVALCANTE:	All right. So how about Joe? Joe knows better than this. This guy's only a *capo*, Joe is supposed to be chief justice—one of the chief justices . . . Now he puts this guy on the shelf—so why shouldn't the Commission put Joe Bonanno on the shelf? You understand?

[*After further discussion*]

ZICARELLI:	. . . Maybe there's something here that you and I don't know about.
DE CAVALCANTE:	I know a little more, Joe. There's a lot of questions they want to ask. Some of them are pretty serious . . . So they wanted me to go back and tell him and to tell these *caporegimes* in his administration that we recognize you but not him. "Don't let this man lead you to where you're all involved. This man has made a mistake." It's a bad situation and I've stuck my neck out all the way, Joe . . .

[*Later*]

DE CAVALCANTE:	I want to tell you something, Joe. You're a *soldier*.
ZICARELLI:	That's all I am!
DE CAVALCANTE:	You see—these people—none of them want to open their mouth about him. There isn't one man in that group that'll challenge him . . . I feel sorry for the situation.
ZICARELLI:	What do you mean, there isn't one man in *our* group?
DE CAVALCANTE:	In your own administration . . . Well, I sat down with

	four or five of them and the best I got was hello and good-bye. The rest of them are at attention.
ZICARELLI:	It could be that they're 100 percent loyal to their boss and they want to stay with him.

[*Later*]

DE CAVALCANTE:	The Commission is satisfied that he don't want to talk to his administration.
ZICARELLI:	He's convinced they would dethrone him?
DE CAVALCANTE:	This—and why don't he want to come up in front of the Commission?

[*After further conversation and some inaudible remarks*]

DE CAVALCANTE:	The Commission can go against it. See in Magliocco's family. They had trouble in there.
ZICARELLI:	When?
DE CAVALCANTE:	Joe Profaci.
ZICARELLI:	Oh, Profaci, yeah.
DE CAVALCANTE:	The Commission went in there and took the family over. When Profaci died, Joe Magliocco took over as Boss. They threw him right out! "Who the hell are you to take over a *borgata*?" He's lucky they didn't kill him! And Signor Bonanno knows this. When we had trouble in our outfit, they came right in: "You people belong to the Commission until this is straightened out." They done the same thing in Pittsburgh. They made the Boss John—uh—
ZICARELLI:	La Rocca.
DE CAVALCANTE:	La Rocca . . . step down—
ZICARELLI:	He's no more boss?
DE CAVALCANTE:	Oh, it's all straightened out now. But Joe Bonanno was in on that deal. They made La Rocca take orders from the Commission until everything was straightened out . . . So, do you understand, Joe? If these people don't enforce what's right and what's wrong, then what's the use of having the Commission?

[*Later*]

DE CAVALCANTE:	Another thing—they're not going to accept his kid (Bill Bonanno) as *consiglieri* . . .[19]

De Cavalcante mentions selection of members of the Commission in the fourth conversation. According to the FBI, Frank Majuri is de Cavalcante's underboss.

Conversation #4
Place: The same
Date: October 16, 1964
Participants: Samuel de Cavalcante and Frank Majuri
Source: FBI Airtel to Director, FBI, from Special Agent in Charge, Newark, November 25, 1964. Italicized portions were translated by the FBI from the Sicilian.

[*After other conversation*]

MAJURI: How can they make a guy like Joe Colombo sit at that Commission? He sits on the Commission too, right?

DE CAVALCANTE: Yeah.

MAJURI: But this is ridiculous, Sam, just because a guy like— well now he's gonna take his (Bonanno's) place, right?

DE CAVALCANTE: First of all—you see—the Commission is all out of order . . . Every five years they're all supposed to retire and all the bosses make guys on the Commission. Understand what I mean? . . . Now where's a guy even like Chicago (Samuel Giancana)—where does he fit in the Commission. You hear this guy talk and he's a nice guy. You can enjoy his company. But he's a jokester! "Hit him! Hit him!" That's all you hear from this guy. He's a guy you could go out and have fun with, *get him drunk,* everything goes. How can he . . . *in the Cosa Nostra.*[20]

In the fifth conversation, de Cavalcante and Joe Zicarelli again discuss the Commission's role and powers; de Cavalcante also points out to Zicarelli that if he were a capo, the position would give him some access to others that he does not now have.

Conversation #5
Place: The same

Date: December 21, 1964
Participants: Samuel de Cavalcante and Joe Zicarelli
Source: FBI airtel to Director, FBI, from Special Agent in Charge,
Newark, December 23, 1964

DE CAVALCANTE: Joe, you don't know the strength of the Commis-
                  sion . . . As long as I'm doing the right thing with my
                  people and they're satisfied, the Commission has no
                  jurisdiction to start anything. They can say, "Listen
                  we made this many laws." They make lots of them,
                  but they can't mix in. But when there's trouble in an
                  outfit or . . .
ZICARELLI: But there was no trouble . . .
DE CAVALCANTE: Wait a minute—or when the head of an outfit is doing
                  the wrong thing. You understand what I mean?
ZICARELLI: Fine—I understand that.
DE CAVALCANTE: So they pull him in. It's just like if Joe Bonanno sent
                  for you, you wouldn't ask "Why does he want me?"
ZICARELLI: I'd have to go.
DE CAVALCANTE: Even if your *caporegime* said no, he's your boss, you
                  would have to go. And it's the same thing, the Com-
                  mission is his boss, not individually, but as a Com-
                  mission.

[*Sam and Joe discuss a man named Joe Natale*]

DE CAVALCANTE: You got to admire him—he wanted to be loyal but—
ZICARELLI: You got to use common sense.
DE CAVALCANTE: You've got twelve men—what's he got—twelve men,
                  fourteen men in his *regime*?
ZICARELLI: He's got about twenty I guess . . . there's twelve or
                  thirteen of them that don't recognize him (Natale)
                  and they want somebody to represent them and take
                  the *regime* over . . . the men run to me.
DE CAVALCANTE: Because you're level headed, that's why.
ZICARELLI: I don't have to be a *caporegime*. They run to me any-
                  how.
DE CAVALCANTE: You could help them more as a *caporegime* because
                  then you've got a position. You could go up to an-
                  other person without asking for representation. You
                  represent yourself . . .

ZICARELLI: These guys—our *decine* is all over New York, Bronx, Brooklyn, downtown, uptown all around . . .

[*The radio is playing*]

DE CAVALCANTE: I don't put this thing on for annoyance. You know in case there's anything—

ZICARELLI: I know. I do that myself. You know if you talk lower than that and there's a bug in the joint they won't get the conversation. If you talk higher than that they will.[21]

In the next conversation, we find that apparently the Commission suspected Bonanno of killing (hitting) someone, and also of attempting to "take over" California.

Conversation # 6
Place: The same
Date: February 2, 1965
Participants: Samuel de Cavalcante and Joseph La Selva
Source: FBI airtel to the Director, FBI, from Special Agent in Charge, Newark, February 3, 1965

[*Discussing the Bonano family; Joseph Bonanno has been removed as boss*]

DE CAVALCANTE: See, Gasparino (Gaspare di Gregorio) looks like the favorite to be the boss. He's got the Commission behind him . . . (Bonanno) put Magliocco up to a lot of things . . . like to kill Carl.

LA SELVA: Well, Magliocco that was his son's father-in-law.

DE CAVALCANTE: He put him up to hit Carl and Tommy Brown (Thomas Lucchese).

LA SELVA: Well, that must have had something to do with Profaci's outfit?

DE CAVALCANTE: Yeah. Now they feel that he poisoned Magliocco. Magliocco didn't die a natural death. Because the only one who could accuse him (of plotting against Gambino and Lucchese) was Magliocco. See Magliocco confessed to it. But this Joe didn't know how far he went. Understand? So they suspect he used a pill on him—that he's noted for it. So he knows the truth of all the damage he done. But they feel he don't know

LA SELVA:

DE CAVALCANTE:

how much the other people know. He's come in and deny everything but he knows he couldn't deny he made people when the books were closed.

LA SELVA: Out on the coast there was some friction, wasn't there?

DE CAVALCANTE: Well, he tried to take California over when they were having trouble. He sent the kid out there with forty guys. The Commission stopped him and that's where the trouble started. If he'd have listened to me that time I went to talk to him—this thing would have been all straightened out. They would have just bawled him out.

LA SELVA: It's a shame. What was he, 58–59 years old and the prestige he had! What was he looking for anyway? It's really bad for the morale of our thing, you know? When they make the rules and then break them themselves. He's been in 20 years.

DE CAVALCANTE: 33 years he's been in.[22]

The seventh conversation is one of several in the transcripts in which the participants express surprise or dismay at the amount of information the press has about them. De Cavalcante, on this occasion as on others not quoted here, comments on the extent to which the Commission is controlled by a few of its members.

Conversation #7
Place: The same
Date: February 24 or 26, 1965
Participants: Samuel de Cavalcante and Lou Larasso
Source: FBI airtel to Director, FBI, from Special Agent in Charge, Newark, March 4, 1965

[*Larasso is explaining an article from the* New York Daily News *reporting on a January, 1965, meeting at the Villa Capri*]

LARASSO: It was like somebody sat down and told them the story. The only thing—they had that Mooney (Samuel Giancana) was there. And he wasn't there.

DE CAVALCANTE: No, he wasn't there.

LARASSO:	Jerry (Gerardo Catena) was there. Tommy Ryan (Thomas Eboli) was there.
DE CAVALCANTE:	Well, we went in together . . . The last time he (Giancana) was down it was at somebody's house.
LARASSO:	Well, they claimed he was there that day.
DE CAVALCANTE:	Of course, Mooney got disgusted. He said, "This Commission! Sometimes I don't know how they run it! To hell with him (reference probably to Joseph Bonanno). As far as I'm concerned—do what you want to do." Now Tommy Brown (Thomas Lucchese) has got the vote from Mooney—and Joe Zerilli. Ange (Bruno) will do what Don Stephano (Magaddino) tells him . . . And Joe Colombo is like an echo for Carlo (Gambino). It was a three-man thing, understand what I mean?[23]

In the eighth conversation, Anthony Russo notes that some members are unable to make a living in illegal gambling or legitimate activities and turn to activities that he considers undesirable—armed robbery, handling narcotics (even though they are not supposed to handle narcotics). Also, de Cavalcante has one person who is not a caporegime but who reports directly to him.

Conversation # 8
Place: The same
Date: May 24, 1965
Participants: Samuel de Cavalcante and Anthony Russo
Source: FBI airtel to the Director, FBI, from Special Agent in Charge, Newark, June 9, 1965

DE CAVALCANTE:	You know Frank (Cocchiaro) is a rough guy that I have to watch. Frank would do heist jobs (armed robberies) if I'd let him.
RUSSO:	Sammy, do you know how many friends of ours are on heists?
DE CAVALCANTE:	They can't support themselves.
RUSSO:	Do you know how many guys in Chicago are peeling (safe-cracking). Do you know how many friends of ours in New York that made it peeling. What they

gonna do. Half these guys are handling junk (narcotics). Now there's a (Cosa Nostra) law out that they can't touch it. They have no other way of making a living so what can they do? All right, we're fortunate enough that we moved around and didn't have to resort to that stuff. We had legitimate things going as well as horses, numbers and everything. Do you know how many deadheads that we take for them (New York family bosses)? . . . Guys are coming to me asking to be put on (work gambling games) and they're friends of ours so I put them on because I can't let them starve to death. Sam, pretty soon I may have to say no to them because I gotta look out for myself. "I'll help your boys when I can."

DE CAVALCANTE: If you can't help them then I will. My people won't starve to death. I'd feed them.

RUSSO: Right. You won't let them because you're their boss. You throw them a few dollars when they need help. You should get a piece of your guys that are making money and don't be the big-hearted guy you've been. I don't have much respect for Lou (Larasso) who was under Nick (Delmore). Who's he under now?

DE CAVALCANTE: He's not under anybody but me and only answers to me.[24]

The ninth conversation is the only one mentioning an underboss; it is interesting that as the problems in the Bonanno family become resolved, Zicarelli is informed who his captain now is, and who the boss and underboss of the family are. Zicarelli would like to be a member of de Cavalcante's family instead of the Bonanno family, and de Cavalcante would like to have him. The Bonanno family apparently had subgroups in Canada and Arizona, and the participants discuss possible assignment of these subgroups to other families. Mike Sabella has violated rules, good manners, prudence, or perhaps all three by sending someone who is not even an *amico nos* to see Frank Majuri, de Cavalcante's underboss.

Conversation #9
Place: The same

Date: June 10, 1965
Participants: Samuel de Cavalcante and Joe Zicarelli
Source: FBI airtel to the Director, FBI, from Special Agent in Charge,
Newark, June 17, 1965

[*Zicarelli would like to be transferred from the Bonanno family, of which Gregorio is now boss, to de Cavalcante's family.*]

ZICARELLI: I went there yesterday. And I think I didn't do myself any good . . . (Zicarelli reports on a conversation with Gaspar di Gregorio) . . . Most of what he said I couldn't understand. He was talking indirectly—not telling me to do anything. And then we left.

DE CAVALCANTE: Didn't he tell what the set-up is?

ZICARELLI: The only thing he told me is, "Mike is your captain."

DE CAVALCANTE: Mike didn't say nothing to you?

ZICARELLI: Mike told me he was my captain too.

DE CAVALCANTE: Well didn't he tell you who the boss is, who the underboss is?

ZICARELLI: Oh yeah. He told me. I congratulated Gaspar . . .

DE CAVALCANTE: Well, they ain't gonna do nothing to you (for asking). See—I was talking to Carl (Gambino) yesterday. And he was telling me what has taken place—Pete's the underboss. He had the list of all the *caporegimes.* So I said, "The only person I'm interested in is Joe." He said, "Just now don't do nothing" . . . You know they were gonna give the guys in Canada away to Buffalo (Magaddino family) . . . He said, "They were gonna give the guys in Arizona to Simone (Frank de Simone)—now Gaspar doesn't want to give nothing away" . . . Carl said, "Aren't you and Joe partners?" I said, "Joe and I don't have to be partners—he can have everything I got." He said, "Sam, Gaspar told me he's gonna keep Joe. He'll probably want Joe close to him."

ZICARELLI: Well if it does happen, I don't know how good it's gonna be. He speaks one language and I speak another. I can't understand him.

DE CAVALCANTE: He said, "You know Joe's a producer." I said, "I don't want him because of that. I want him because he's a sincere guy and I don't want him to have a hard time." He said, "What makes you think he'll have a hard time?" I said, "Well, he's always around here—I need Joe. You know what I got over there . . ." He (Gambino) said, "Gaspar knows how close you are."

ZICARELLI: Yeah, he does—but what good is it?

DE CAVALCANTE: Now with Mike Sabella—what do you think of that?

ZICARELLI: They made him a captain.

DE CAVALCANTE: Well what do you think of him sending that guy to Frank (Majuri). Frank said this guy isn't even an *amico nos.*[25]

The tenth conversation confirms that Carl Gambino is the boss of a family and has fired his underboss, in much the same way anyone can lose a job. The position is vacant.

Conversation #10
Place: The same
Date: June 10, 1965
Participants: Samuel de Cavalcante, Lou Larasso, and Mickey Puglio
Source: FBI airtel to the Director, FBI, from Special Agent in Charge, Newark, June 17, 1965

LARASSO: How about Joe (Zicarelli)?

DE CAVALCANTE: I'm gonna try to grab him.

LARASSO: With us?

DE CAVALCANTE: Yeah. But I don't think it's gonna work out. This guy (Gaspar) was very liberal when he needed everybody. He was gonna give Canada to Niagara Falls—he was gonna give Arizona to California . . .

LARASSO: He was gonna give New Jersey to . . .

DE CAVALCANTE: (Facetiously) . . . to the Indians . . . but once he got in he ain't giving anything up. (To Mickey) Do you know Gasparino?

PUGLIO: No.

DE CAVALCANTE: He took Bonanno's place. It's official now. It's also official that Joe Bandy (Joseph Biondo) is not no more the underboss for Carl (Gambino).

PUGLIO: He wanted a new man, or what?

DE CAVALCANTE:	He hasn't picked anybody yet.
PUGLIO:	He's (Biondo) still in the family?
DE CAVALCANTE:	There hasn't been nothing said, but (Joseph) Zingaro is still *caporegime*.[26]

In the eleventh conversation, we find that de Cavalcante has certain standards of behavior for *amico nos* and caporegimes. That those with positions in the hierarchy should set an example for others is a common theme in the transcripts.

Conversation #11
Place: The same
Date: June 11, 1965
Participants: Samuel de Cavalcante and Lou Larasso
Source: FBI memorandum to Special Agent in Charge, Newark, from Clerk William P. Nugent, July 6, 1965

DE CAVALCANTE:	You know how Sferra broke his leg. He was taking his daughter home from school and there were three other girls from her school with them. So, he gets behind this young kid who's got a broad in the car almost sitting on his lap. Sferra gets mad at this and goes around this kid's car cutting him off. The kid chases after him and when Joe stops at a light, both of them got out of the car. Joe berates the kid and words are exchanged until Joe pushed the kid. The kid went after him like a tiger and puts Joe off his feet. When he fell, he broke his foot. Now, is this any way for an *amico nos* and a *caporegime* to act?
LARASSO:	No.[27]

In the twelfth conversation, de Cavalcante is apparently trying to explain to people from another family that as far as he is concerned, they can expect the same treatment from members of his family as the members receive from each other.

Conversation #12
Place: The same
Date: June 16, 1965

Participants: Samuel de Cavalcante, Tony (last name unknown), and an
unidentified male
Source: FBI airtel to the Director, FBI, from Special Agent in Charge,
New York, July 2, 1965. Translated, probably from the Sicilian, by the
FBI.

DE CAVALCANTE: . . . there is no difference between you and Joe and
our people. When you people are here you are re-
spected like our people. Tomorrow if you need anything you can come here. You can "captain" your own
people. You understand what I mean? You will be
treated like anyone else is treated here. The way we
do it also goes for you. Respect for you belonging to
another family, you don't have to tell me anything.
If you need money we will give it to you, we will
respect you as an *amico nostro* . . . *Cosa Nostra* is *Cosa
Nostra* (our thing is our thing). I can only speak for
my people, but not for anyone else. When you call the
family for your own intention, an *amico nostro* is an
amico nostro. If he belongs here or there it doesn't mean
a thing, if you give me preference I will also give you
preference . . . The *Cosa Nostra* has become a public
thing as far as I am concerned.[28]

It is not surprising that the structure of Italian organized criminal
groups, as one can infer it from the de Cavalcante Transcripts, is so consistent with the description given by writers such as Cressey and Salerno.
Cressey interviewed many officials of the FBI and the Organized Crime
and Racketeering Section of the U.S. Department of Justice when doing
research for his book, and they had been reading transcripts of electronic
surveillance on organized crime figures for years. Joseph Valachi's
congressional testimony provided the same information; but for the U.S.
Department of Justice the importance of the testimony lay not in the
information provided, but in the fact that Valachi was a means of
making public what law enforcement officials were then beginning to
find out, or already knew, from wiretaps and microphones. The
existence of an organization hierarchy within groups does not mean that
all activities, legal and illegal, business and social, of the members are
necessarily subject to control of the hierarchy. In fact, the de Cavalcante
Transcripts do not support statements about organized crime that it is

totalitarian in organization, that its structure is as complex as that of any large corporation, or that its laws are more rigidly enforced than those of legitimate governments.

It is not clear from the de Cavalcante Transcripts exactly what the powers of the Commission are. De Cavalcante seems to think that the Commission has a very limited role or jurisdiction over the affairs of a particular family unless there is a problem within the family: if the boss, for example, is not treating members of the family as he should. But the quotations suggest that the real reason the members of the Commission decided to do something about Bonanno was that he was plotting against some of them. If administrations of families can be compared to governments, the Commission would by analogy be composed of selected heads of state, or it would be a body comparable to the United Nations. The Commission has no police or military powers in place, and it meets essentially on matters of relations among families rather than within them—negotiating to avoid war when it can, declaring war when necessary. While this interpretation is at least consistent with the de Cavalcante Transcripts, the transcripts nevertheless provide only a partial insight into the structure of Italian-American organized criminal groups and relations within and among them—and none whatsoever into the importance of the Italian groups in organized crime in the United States.

Neither the existence of a commission nor business and social relations among members of different groups demonstrates that a national syndicate controls the activities of individual groups; and that argument is not being made here. The matters over which the Commission has authority may be quite limited and its powers to carry out its decisions even more so. According to de Cavalcante, the Commission has temporarily taken over a family with internal problems on several occasions; but the transcripts do not throw much light on what the Commission actually does, or what it controls, when it takes over a family.

A reading of the entire document shows that a great deal of de Cavalcante's time and that of his associates is spent in talking about problems of leadership and control of members who talk too much, engage in activities that endanger others, take too big a cut from others' businesses, borrow too much, don't pay debts, and cheat one another. The transcripts also show that the leaders of the group take some responsibility for the jobs and income of members. Murray Kempton, who attemped an overall analysis of the documents, noted that in terms of jobs and income, the local hodcarriers' union was more valuable than the numbers racket.[29]

II

THE BENGUERRA FAMILY

The Benguerra family has a hierarchical organization structure similar to that described as characteristic of Italian organized criminal groups by Cressey and Salerno and apparent in the de Cavalcante Transcripts, quoted in Chapter I. Its formal organization structure is not, however, the same as its economic structure. The group is not a firm, that is, a business enterprise owned and controlled as a unit. Instead, the group has within it several firms involved in numbers gambling and several in loansharking. Some of the members who do not hold positions in the hierarchy have larger illegal market businesses than those who do.

Formally the Benguerra family's organization structure includes the following positions: boss, underboss, counselor, treasurer, and ten caporegimes or capos (heads of groups). Under the capos are the lowest-ranking members. The structure is shown in Figure 1.

The underboss position in organized criminal groups has sometimes been described as a vice presidency, but the term used in government organizations is more accurate: the underboss is a deputy; he takes over the functions and powers of the boss when the boss is out of town.

The counselor position is considered by Cressey to be an advisory role in organized criminal groups and not a line position.[1] Line authority goes through the underboss to the capos. A counselor is usually an older, experienced, perhaps retired member who advises the boss. In the Benguerra family, however, the counselor, while older and experienced, appears to do very little counseling. And he is also a capo with his own regime. The counselor and many members of his regime and of one of the other regimes are Calabrians from southern Italy; most other members of the group are Sicilians. The distinction is apparently im-

FIGURE 1

THE ORGANIZATION STRUCTURE OF THE
BENGUERRA FAMILY

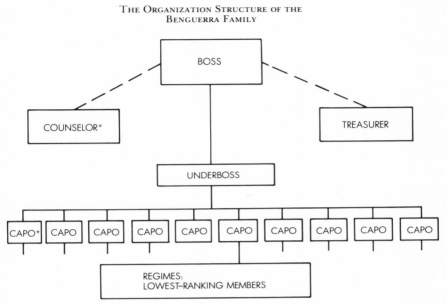

*These positions are occupied by the same individual.

portant, because it has led to two power blocs in the group, the larger
Sicilian group and the minority Calabrian group.

The boss of the group may have recognized this situation as a
potential problem and decided to give representation at the highest level
possible to the minority power block without increasing the line authority of the senior member of that group. As counselor, the Calabrian capo
has the right of direct access to the boss, although it is doubtful that he
sees the boss any oftener than other capos—perhaps less often.

The group also has a treasurer. Some or all of the members pay dues,
in small amounts—perhaps $10 to $25 per year. This money is collected
by the capos from the members, given to the treasurer, and used to pay
for some legal expenses, to make loans to members for legal expenses,
and to pay for items such as flowers for funerals.

One of the capos is especially close to the boss and operates a major
illegal enterprise for the boss and other backers. Except for this capo
and the people who work with him in this illegal enterprise, there is no
staff to carry out personal orders or protect the boss, as one might

expect to find in an analogy with a military or paramilitary organization.

The boss of the Benguerra family selects the people who hold the various positions in the hierarchy. They can be demoted, but this occurs rarely; they are more likely to be gradually shifted aside so that they have few people under them. Members of the group can resign from positions of authority, usually for reasons of ill health. They can also turn down promotions, and sometimes they do; whenever this has occurred, the person offered the job has had legitimate business interests to pursue.

Finally, the group has contacts with the Commission. It sends money, the purpose of which is unknown, to the Commission. The money may represent dues payments or, as the data sources suggest, payments for police protection; but it is also possible that the Commission functions as a central group for raising and investing funds from and for the various groups.

Clearly, the organization structure of the Benguerra family is not as complex as that of any large corporation—as the task force of the President's Commission on Law Enforcement and Administration of Justice claims such structures are.[2] It is, however, more defined and formal than Ianni claims: "Secret criminal groups such as *Mafia* are . . . traditional social systems . . . that are structured by action rather than by a series of statuses and . . . have no structure apart from their functioning."[3] Positions in the Benguerra family hierarchy can be vacant; appointments can be refused; incumbents can resign.

Cressey points out that a formal organization structure does not tell us what functions are performed by members of a group, nor does it touch on their relations with outsiders (public officials, attorneys, nonmember employees in illegal market enterprises) or the roles that need to be filled by such outsiders. He suggests several functional positions: money mover, enforcer, executioner, corrupter, and corruptee. These are positions of expertise that he considers essential to the functioning of an organized criminal group, although the individuals who hold these positions may not be members of the group. The role of enforcer, for example, is to arrange, when ordered to do so, the killing or maiming of members and sometimes nonmembers; the role of executioner is to actually do the killing or maiming.[4]

Five or six members of the Benguerra family or their close associates fulfill Cressey's description of the executioner role. They are sometimes also hired by outsiders. For all of them, the executioner role is only occasional, and thus they cannot be considered analagous to a full-time police force or army. Members of the group were suspects in four murders and four beatings (or assaults) of nonmembers during the 1960s. In at least two of these cases, the victim was murdered or beaten to prevent or discourage his talking about other predatory activities in which he had taken part with members of the group. One of the victims of a beating was a loanshark borrower.

In at least two of these cases and perhaps all of them, the use of violence was sanctioned by the boss. External violence may thus require the permission of the boss. At one time a member in legitimate business wished to use violence to discourage competition from a nearby retail enterprise in a legal industry but was not permitted to do so. Internal violence appears to be nonexistent (although two members of the group disappeared during the 1960s), and members are supposed to avoid competition among themselves. The top-level members of the group arbitrate disputes among members that cannot be resolved at lower levels.

The leaders of the group—those with positions above the lowest-ranking members, and especially the boss—also have some responsibility for helping members make a living. When members are having difficulty, the boss and other ranking members will try to find jobs for them or assist them with illegal activities. The leaders also try to protect the group and their businesses by finding jobs for members and associates who are judged too "hot," in the sense of police attention, or too hot-headed, to be active in illegal market enterprises or legitimate businesses owned and operated by members of the group.

The permission of the boss is required for all gambling ventures—numbers, bookmaking, and casino-type gambling (craps and cards). Other activities, selling stolen goods, for example, are supposed to be reported by the member to his capo. Four activities are allegedly forbidden: kidnapping, white slave traffic, counterfeiting, and narcotics traffic. (Four of the members have arrests for narcotics, all prior to 1960. The two members in jail during the 1968–1969 period were there on narcotics convictions.) In addition, members have been advised against selling stolen goods, although some of them do so at times.

A major service the Benguerra family performs for its members is that of corruption. Corruption is apparently the responsibility of the boss, although he may at times ask the assistance of a member who has contact with a particular individual, or with a member of another criminal group who has useful contacts. Sometimes payment is in kind rather than cash—the outside criminal fixes a problem for the group, and they fix a problem for the outsider. The boss's contacts appear weakest with labor unions, where he uses the contacts of other members.

The group or its top leaders also loan money to members to pay fines and legal fees resulting from law enforcement action, and sometimes for other purposes. Cressey reports that the boss of a Cosa Nostra family is said to have given $100,000 to each of five lieutenants, who were obligated to pay him $150,000 within a year. The lieutenants, who planned to invest the money in loansharking, are supposed to have been delighted.[5] This example suggests that internal lending rates—in this case, 50 percent a year—would be useful to examine. If members are willing to borrow at high rates of interest, the assumption must be that they are able to earn an even higher rate of return on the funds borrowed.

However, internal loans within the Benguerra family are interest-free. This appears to be the case even among those who could pay higher rates, although in such cases the possibility arises that the money was being held for the presumed borrower and actually belonged to him. Thus internal lending rates offer no clue to rates of return on illegal enterprises. Internal lending is instead a service provided by the group as a quasi-governmental function.

Loans within the Benguerra family are predominately for two purposes: to pay gambling debts and to pay legal fees associated with arrests. The amounts vary from a few hundred dollars to perhaps $5,000. Payment periods may be as long as a year, even when repayment requires only $25 per week. With occasional exceptions, the borrowers are less successful members of the group; the lenders are wealthy individuals also involved in loansharking. The borrower must have the approval of his capo or superior in the organization, who may be surety for the loan. When members do not repay loans on schedule, the lender may appeal to the surety. The resulting decisions are sometimes based on the ability of the borrower to repay and the lender's need for the money.

Loans are not made for the purpose of financing a numbers or loansharking enterprise. Instead, the wealthier members finance the enterprise and receive a percentage of some kind, a procedure that allows the operator of the business to develop his own capabilities and perhaps eventually become independent. Control of the supply of funds is one of the group's major means of control of its less successful members.

The leadership of the Benguerra family also maintains relations with other organized criminal groups in the city. The Benguerra family is the only such Italian group, but there are two other groups of different ethnic minority backgrounds in the city, smaller and with less well-defined identification of members and nonmembers. Although the information is limited, the three groups appear to have some division of territory worked out, at least for purposes of gambling. The Italian group is unchallenged in one section of the city, a section bordered on one side by the city's central business district and otherwise defined by natural boundaries such as rivers. Census tract data for 1970 were used to determine the population and ethnic makeup of this section. The population is about 230,000. Although the section is sometimes informally referred to as the Italian section, its population is approximately 30 percent Black and 20 percent Italian.[6] In addition, some members of the Italian group live in surrounding smaller cities that are within commuting distance, engaging there in various legal and illegal enterprises.

Like the Italian group, one of the other groups is involved in numbers gambling, an illegal lottery. The third group, unlike the Italian one, handles bookmaking; only occasionally do members of the Italian group engage in bookmaking. The group in bookmaking and the Italian group both have contacts in the city government and especially in the criminal justice system—in other words, corruptees—and sometimes assist each other when one needs the help of someone with whom the other has contact. There is also mutual investment in some legitimate businesses among the members of these two groups. Both groups are involved in loansharking.

There is evidence that the Benguerra family has declined in size since Prohibition days and will decline further if its past recruitment pattern continues. As of 1970, the group had 75 members. In addition, it was possible to identify from the data sources a considerable number of associates, sixteen of them close, of the group. The most important associates can be placed in the following categories:

Category A (close) associates. The category A associate fulfills the basic requirement for membership in the group in that he is of Italian national origin. He may aspire to membership, or he may have been considered for membership in the past and been rejected. He is actively engaged in the activities of the group, either in illegal markets or legitimate business, and associates closely with two or more members. If he is engaged in legal activities, he has firsthand knowledge of the group's illegal activities. In short, he is an associate of the group rather than of an individual member and probably gets many, but not all, benefits of membership.

Category B associates. The category B associate may or may not fulfill membership eligibility requirements. He works for one member of the group as an employee, usually in illegal activities such as gambling or loansharking. Insofar as he is protected from the activities of law enforcement officials, he is protected by the individual who employs him and not by the group.

Category C associates. The category C associate may, in rare cases, fulfill membership eligibility requirements, but he probably does not. He manages, as a professional, a legitimate business financed by members of the organized criminal group. Although he may be a dishonest business-man and may at times be required by the group to operate the business in an illegal or unethical manner, or may do so on his own, he is basically a businessman rather than a gangster. The owners of the business, of which he may be one, depend on his professional skills to make the business successful.

Category D associates. The category D associate is the professional lawyer, accountant, or bail bondsman whose main clients are the members of the organized criminal group, and the businessman who deals with members of organized criminal groups. Also included in this category are co-investors in legitimate business who function as equals with the investing members of the group. They may manage the businesses in which they are co-investors, but as equals rather than employees.

Other categories of associates could also be set up: corruptees, girl-friends, nonmember relatives who do not fit in one of the above categories. The categories obviously merge, and an associate might move from one category to another over time.

Category A associates have been included in the analyses of illegal market activities and legitimate business holdings because they are people who might become members if the Benguerra family chose to take in new members and was permitted by the Commission to do so. Some of them may already be members. Others may have been rejected for membership or may not wish to join, but may still function as do members in operating illegal markets and investing in legitimate businesses.

Figure 2 shows the age distribution of the group's 75 members. The ages of five members are estimates based on information such as the length of time the individual has owned a legitimate business or the age of other members of his immediate family. In one case two birthdates were given for an individual; the later year was selected as the most likely. For five members, ages are simply unknown. Of the group's sixteen close associates, one is over 60. The ages of the others are not known, but they are probably under 60.

The advanced age of many of the members is striking: the median age of living members is 60 years. (Median calculations are based on actual ages rather than the consolidated categories.) Thus 30 years ago, the number of men under the current median age must have been considerably larger than it is now, if it is assumed that new members are young (under 30). But this has not been the case in the last several years. Of the seventeen men reported by informants to have been inducted into the group in the years 1958–1969, eight were 45 or over at the time of induction. Nine were under 45, and six were 25 to 34. These six are among the eight members of the group who were between 35 and 44 in 1969. One of the remaining two was inducted before 1968; the induction date of the other is unknown. The age of an eighteenth individual inducted during that period is unknown.

The induction information is not completely reliable; the bias is such that individuals may have become members earlier than indicated. More members may have been inducted during this period also, possibly including some of the associates. If one of the associates is over 60 and the others are evenly distributed from 35 to 59, the median age of members and associates is still 58 years.

Many members of the group could have been active during Prohibition; several were part of a Prohibition gang. The 23 people aged 65 and over in 1969 were young adults during Prohibition, and the 25 people aged 55 to 64 reached young adulthood then; all 48 could therefore have been active in the illegal liquor trade. The latter group would have been only 5–14 years old when Prohibition began in 1919 and 19–28 when it ended in 1933. Four of them (those inducted at an age over 50) did not, however, become members until 1958 or after. The overall picture is of a group that received its impetus for existence during Prohibition and, whatever interim peaks in strength it may have

FIGURE 2

AGE DISTRIBUTION OF 75 MEMBERS OF THE BENGUERRA FAMILY, 1969

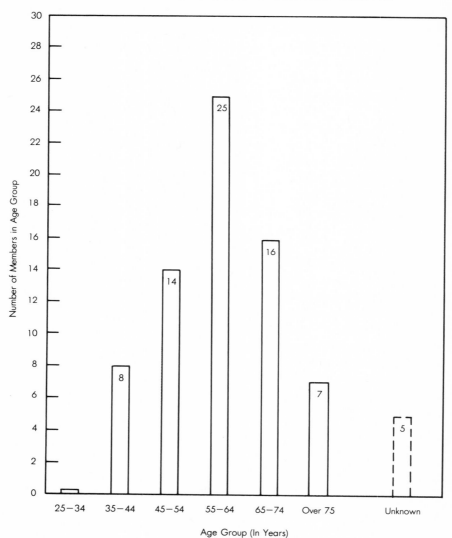

reached, is now aging and declining in total membership.

What will happen to the size of the group as of 1979 and 1989 if it follows its 1958—1968* recruitment pattern in the years 1969—1978 and 1979—1988? If the induction pattern is repeated until current members no longer influence the number and age distribution, the result is 38 members under 65 and 53 under 75 years of age. The current pattern of recruitment is not sufficient to maintain the size of the group, which in 1969 had 47 members under 65 and 63 under 75, plus the five members whose ages are unknown.

The recruiting pattern would give the following results as of 1979 and 1989:

	1969	1979	1989
Members aged 25–34	0	3	3
Members aged 35–44	8	5	8
Members aged 45–54	14	12	9
Members aged 55–64	25	19	17
Total under 65	47	39	37
Members aged 65–74	16	25	19
Total under 75	63	64	56

If the group inducts members in the future at the rate and of the ages it has in the past, it will decline in number of members under age 65 from 47 in 1969 to 39 in 1979 and 37 in 1989. These calculations do not allow for the death of older members as would an actuarial analysis; an actuarial analysis would also enable the membership decline to be extended into the past. The evidence for decline in the size of the group is stronger in view of the fact that members of organized criminal groups probably have a higher than average rate of death from unnatural causes than the general population. The number of gangland killings that occurred in this group prior to 1958 is not known, but some did occur. Since 1958 no members of the group are known to have been murdered, but two have disappeared.

If the number of members of the group is declining, the total number of members and close associates is probably declining also. A declining group would be expected to have fewer close associates than an expanding group of the same size, which would need close associates from whom to recruit new members. An offsetting possibility is that

---

*The year 1958 is included as a means of substituting the age of the individual inducted in that year for the unknown age of the individual actually inducted between 1959 and 1968.

close associates are carrying out more of the group's activities than formerly—especially illegal activities.

I also analyzed data on the ages of 54 members and close associates of another Italian organized criminal group. The list of members and associates was not all-inclusive, and induction information was not available. The data (for 1970) showed one member under 25 years of age; two of 25–34 years; twelve of 35–44 years; eleven of 45–54 years; fifteen of 55–64; ten of 65–74 years; two over 75 years; and one whose age was unknown. This is a somewhat younger age distribution than that of the Benguerra family; the median age is 55.[7]

The criminal firm operating in an illegal market is in a very different position from a legitimate business firm. Ownership of the firm is not legally recognized and thus cannot be legally transferred. The owners of the criminal firm cannot enter into legally recognized contractual relationships with outsiders, customers, or their own employees. Owners of the firm (and employees) are subject to arrest and incarceration and thus possibly to the termination of their enterprises as going concerns. Assets may be seized, either by law enforcement officials or other criminals. Finally, entrepreneurs in illegal markets are at risk from the use of information to their detriment by their associates. The comparable problem in the legitimate world—controlling the use employees can make of information—is dealt with through legislation or contract.

The problems of the criminal firm are the problems of a firm operating without the benefits of a legitimate government that defines property rights, adjudicates disputes, and has the power to enforce its decisions. Thus the criminal firm may benefit from a criminal government (or quasi-government) that will do for it what the legitimate government will not: establish and protect (quasi-) property rights, adjudicate disputes, and enforce decisions. An individual entrepreneur may find membership in a larger group desirable; the group may protect his ownership of an illegal enterprise and perhaps keep the business going if he is imprisoned. The group can also limit competition among firms, defining acceptable ("legitimate") competition, and set prices, assign territories, and restrict entry by others—functions of a regulatory agency or cartel. It may also use violence or the threat of violence to enforce contracts. The group can limit the risk individual members pose to other members by controlling the actions of the former so that they do not endanger the latter by discussing illegal activities indiscreetly or using excessive violence.

As later chapters will show, the leadership of the Benguerra family operates in some areas (specifically, numbers gambling) as a cartel. Some of the leaders also operate a wholesale firm with which small retail numbers firms can lay off bets, thus transferring the risk to the larger firm. As Paul Rubin points out, this is an example of economies of scale through the pooling of risks.[8] Corruption and the use of violence in enforcing contracts with customers (for example, in collecting loan-shark debts) may also be matters of economies of scale, and the argument could therefore be made that these services are performed by a firm at the wholesale level.

But the hierarchy of the Benguerra family functions in ways that go beyond those of a cartel or a firm operating at the wholesale level, supplying services to retail firms. It limits the use of violence by members, even when that violence has no relation to a particular illegal market. Members who talk too much are disciplined and moved into jobs where they do not acquire information that could be used to the detriment of other members. The group's leadership controls the use of corruption for the benefit of members in trouble with the authorities and sometimes decides who shall "take the rap" for a particular offense. These are essentially functions of a government. This is not the first time, of course, this observation has been made. Schelling, Cressey, and others have noted and sometimes discussed at length the governmental functions of organized criminal groups.[9]

A basic problem of all rulers and governments is that of legitimating authority or domination, and there is extensive literature in sociology and political theory on the subject.[10] The attempt to legitimate authority is an important sociological characteristic of a quasi-government; economically, a distinguishing characteristic of a governmental function would be that it is undertaken on a nonmarket basis, perhaps unilaterally. Internalizing the external costs of violence by limiting its use, controlling the behavior of members to avoid harm to other members, protecting property rights of members, and deciding when the group's influence over law enforcement shall be used on behalf of a particular person are functions of a government rather than a firm for the following reason: the effective provision of these services requires that the exercise of authority and power in making and carrying out these decisions be viewed by the members as legitimate.

In one case (before the 1960s) the boss of the Benguerra family was given authority by the Commission to murder a member of the group who had attempted to murder him. This is an extreme example, but it does show that members of organized criminal groups distinguish between violence that is "legitimate" and violence that is not; murder that is not legitimate is an act of war. The critical element is that members of the group acknowledge the legitimate authority of the leaders to govern, even when governing means the use of the ultimate sanction of death.

Many groups undertake crimes for economic gain. Some of these crimes involve consensual market transactions (gambling, fencing stolen goods). The crimes may be victimless, involving no harm except the harm inflicted on the parties to the transactions, or they may be predatory, involving a third-party victim. Others are nonmarket crimes—labor racketeering, for example. These groups often exhibit many of the characteristics of a formal organization: as Ianni puts it, a rationally designed structure for achieving specific goals, as well as characteristics such as a division of labor, a hierarchy, a means of communication and perhaps recruitment. The existence of such an organization is perhaps not, however, what makes "organized crime" more threatening than crime that is organized. A great deal of crime is undertaken by groups that fulfill some sociological definition of an organization. What is threatening may be, instead, the group or organization's capacity for forming a quasi-government.

Functioning as a quasi-government may give the group a competitive advantage in illegal markets. But it is likely that a quasi-government can develop only when it is advantageous and when the possibility of legitimating its authority is especially favorable. A factor that can make it easier to legitimate authority is the existence of some basis on which members can identify themselves as part of the group and accept a code of morality that requires different behavior toward members than toward outsiders, expects different behavior from members than from outsiders, and sanctions such behavior. The capability for establishing and maintaining a quasi-government may depend on cultural or sociological factors peculiar to the members of the group; this may explain why organized criminal groups are often made up of a single minority and why Italian organized criminal groups have been more successful than other ethnic groups in organized crime in the last several decades.[11]

The social values and behavioral codes of southern Italians who immigrated to the United States, and from whose ranks members of Italian organized criminal groups have come, may be responsible for the success of Italian organized criminal groups. Ianni analyzed the Italian-American organized criminal group that he studied, called the Lupollo family, as a traditional social system in which the hierarchy is based on a pattern of relationships among individuals and has the force of kinship. He notes that the family he studied is more strongly influenced by kinship ties than most Italian-American organized crime families in terms of family solidarity, exclusion of nonmembers, and preferential treatment of kin. Nevertheless, he is convinced that the centrality of kinship distinguishes such groups from those of earlier ethnic minorities. In support of this tentative conclusion, he presents kinship data on an East Harlem family and on the Detroit organized criminal group; in the latter, all twenty lineages are intermarried and have also intermarried with Italian organized criminal groups in three other cities.

Furthermore, Ianni notes that the pattern of reciprocal rights and obligations based on kinship can be extended beyond blood relationships if the group recruits, provides greater security than the limited kinship relationship of the nuclear family, and develops some symbolism or ritual to replace or extend the concept of blood ties. Behavior in the Lupollo family is governed by three rules: primary loyalty is vested in the extended family rather than in individual lineages or nuclear families; each member must "act like a man" and do nothing to disgrace the family; and family business (illegal and legal) is privileged matter and must not be discussed outside the group.

Finally, Ianni concludes that acculturation to American values is breaking down the values and kinship structure that have solidified the Italian-American crime family. He predicts that utilitarian values—ability rather than ascribed status—will become increasingly important within organized crime families and will ultimately lead to a business structure that is more bureaucratic and more like American corporations; the business structure will no longer be coterminus with the family's social organization. At the same time, the weakening of the family and kinship among Italian-Americans will lead to the succession in organized crime of other ethnic minorities—blacks, Puerto Ricans, Cubans.[12]

Italian organized criminal groups apparently have succeeded in establishing quasi-governments based on a kinship model, and the strength of this approach may have given them an advantage over organized criminal groups of other ethnic minorities. This suggests that organized criminal groups of other or mixed ethnic backgrounds are likely to differ from Italian groups in organization, functioning, and in their means of and capability for survival.[13] Problems arise in two areas: recruitment and succession of leadership.

One of the reasons the Benguerra family may be having difficulty recruiting is that the life of a member of an Italian-American organized criminal group is less attractive, relative to alternatives, than it once was. Many children of members of organized crime families, including the Benguerra and Lupollo families, choose legitimate careers, and what information is available suggests that their member-fathers are proud of them and do not wish them to become members. This is essentially the hypothesis Daniel Bell presented when he said that "the urban rackets—the illicit activity organized for continuing profit, rather than individual illegal acts—is one of the queer ladders of social mobility in American life." Bell traced Irish, Jewish, and finally Italian ethnic succession in organized criminal activity, concluding that "in the major northern urban centers there was a distinct ethnic sequence in the modes of obtaining illicit wealth . . . uniquely in the case of the recent Italian elements, the former bootleggers and gamblers provided considerable leverage for the growth of political influence as well."[14] Bell predicted that with the general rise of minority groups to social position and the breakup of the urban boss system, the pattern of crime he described was passing.

The Benguerra family may consider it necessary to restrict recruiting members of its own ethnic minority in order to maintain its capability for governing. The problem is that young Italian-Americans, especially, in this case, of Sicilian or Calabrian extraction, are often third- or fourth-generation Americans with American values and culture, and are perhaps unwilling to give primary loyalty to the hierarchy of an organized crime family and acknowledge its quasi-governmental authority as legitimate indefinitely. This suggests that even if other opportunities were limited and many people wished to become members, the Italian-American organized criminal group should have increasing difficulty governing.

As with recruitment, the problem of succession is closely related to the problem of governing or of legitimating authority. Unless the means of succession are accepted as legitimate, the new leader's authority may not be accepted. Ianni reports no violence in the process of succession in the Lupollo family; power has been transferred from father to son and will perhaps be transferred to a grandson. For other Italian organized criminal groups, however, succession of leadership has been a major problem and is often, perhaps usually, accompanied by violence.[15]

Cressey attributes the problem of succession to the family structure of organized criminal groups: because the structure is fictional (ties are extended beyond blood relationships), the son cannot inherit the father's domain—but the fiction of kinship prevents the development of an orderly procedure for selecting successors.[16]

Regardless of the basis for the ties that enable the group to form a quasi-government, the problem of succession may be inherent when the organized criminal group as a government is in fact not synonymous or coextensive with the organized criminal group as an economic (or business) organization. In the Benguerra family as in others, the same people make up both organizations. Economic success in an illegal enterprise is no doubt important in achieving a position of leadership within the group; and a position of leadership may be economically advantageous. Nevertheless, the organized criminal group is not a firm, but includes firms within it. As a quasi-government that defines and protects (quasi-) property rights, the leaders are likely to come into conflict with the owners or potential owners of illegal market enterprises. If a single large firm were able to control an illegal market, its owners would be the leaders of the quasi-government, and succession would be based on ownership. But apparently existing illegal markets are too competitive, or economies of scale not great enough, to make this possible. Insofar as the economic and governmental structures of organized criminal groups are separate (although overlapping in personnel), no extra-economic means of determining succession is likely to be successful in eliminating conflict and challenges to authority. Thus the potential for conflict is independent of the particular means the group depends on to establish a government and legitimate authority—whether social and traditional or rational and formal.

III

NUMBERS GAMBLING

A numbers lottery is the major form of gambling in which the Benguerra family is involved. It brings in more money and employs more people than the group's other illegal market enterprise, loansharking.

Illegal numbers lotteries exist in many cities in the United States. Although there are many variations, the basic play is simple: the bettor bets on any three-digit number from 000 to 999. He may, at least in principle, bet any amount he wishes, and any number of bettors may select the same number. Bets can be placed every day of the week except Sunday. The bettor has one chance in 1,000 of winning, but if he wins he may be paid only 500 times the amount of his bet. In the city where the Benguerra family operates, payouts were 600 to 1 in the mid-1960s: a winning bettor received $600 for a $1 bet. Whether they were still that high in 1970—higher than payouts on numbers in many major cities[1]— is not known. Usually, some numbers (those often heavily played) pay less than the basic amount, perhaps 400 to 1 where the basic rate is 600 to 1. The players are generally informed about which numbers are "cut" before they place their bets.

Illegal lotteries are ongoing businesses rather than fly-by-night operations. They have loyal customers and well-developed networks of corruptees in the criminal justice system for protection. Such enterprises are often owned and operated by members of established organized criminal groups.

Numbers gambling may sound like a sinecure for the entrepreneur, but it is not. Gambling games that are run as a business can be placed in two categories: those where the entrepreneur is, like an insurance company, taking a risk of losses greater than the amount bet, and those where he is not. The major example of a gambling enterprise in which the entrepreneur is not taking such a risk is pari-mutuel racetrack betting. Here the race track collects the bets, takes a percentage of the amount bet as an excise tax for the government and a higher percentage as its gross revenue, and simply divides the remaining amount (usually around 85 percent of the amount bet) among the winners in proportion to the amount of their bets.* Profits are not guaranteed: operating expenses and overhead must be covered out of gross revenue.

The other kind of gambling game is one in which the entrepreneur does take the risk of winnings greater than the amount bet. Most casino games are of this type: roulette, craps, blackjack. So is the numbers lottery. In roulette one can place a $2 chip on the red and win $4; no one else may be betting. In the numbers lottery, an entrepreneur can take a bet on, say, 529. There is only one chance in a thousand that 529 will be the winning number, but if it is the entrepreneur owes the bettor $500 or $600. The entrepreneur would be entirely safe if he collected, say, a $1 bet on each number from 000 to 999; he would then be indifferent about the winning number. But bettors have favorite numbers, and some of them may have the same favorite numbers—333, for example, or 734, or the date (529 on May 29), or anything with sevens and sixes during the bicentennial year. Bettors may select any number they wish, even if someone else has also chosen it. The entrepreneur is thus not likely to have his bets distributed uniformly over the thousand possible numbers, and on any given day he faces the risk that more will be won than has been bet—perhaps substantially more.

When the winning three-digit number in a numbers lottery is determined from race track results, the numbers lottery is called a pari-mutuel lottery, but it is not in fact pari-mutuel. Everyone who wins is paid a predetermined multiple of the amount bet. Operators face bankruptcy if they do not maintain capital reserves to pay winners on those days when the amount won exceeds the amount bet.

Another problem faces the numbers operator: that of cheating by employees. The bets are placed, of course, before the winning number is known; but the tabulation of the bets and the determination of winners takes place afterward, and an employee might be able to insert into the

---

*Because the track will always pay a minimum ($2.10 on a $2.00 bet, usually) on winning bets, it may sometimes, if most of the money is bet on the winning horses, have to dip into what would otherwise be its gross revenues to pay the minimum. This is called a negative pool; it is rare, occurring most often on place and show bets.

stack of bets a bet on the winning number, presumably placed by a customer whom the employee does not know. Setting up procedures for ensuring that this does not happen is one of the managerial skills required to run a successful numbers operation.

During the 1968–1969 period, members of the Benguerra family operated fourteen separate retail numbers firms—that is, firms dealing directly with bettors—two of them outside the main city. Of the twelve within the main city, eleven were in that section controlled by the group; the twelfth was outside this area. In addition, two nonmember numbers firms operated in the section of the city controlled by the group. These two and three of the member operators paid a percentage, probably of gross revenues, to a fourth member-operator—either for the privilege to operate, or because this member-operator was handling corruption payments for them. What the percentage was, and whether it was the same for members and nonmembers, is not known.

Information on amounts bet with the fourteen firms is limited; but the amounts varied considerably. One of the member-operated enterprises in the city was taking in only about $50 a week or less in bets. Two others were taking in about $1,000 a week each. I estimated another to be small, with total amounts bet of $2,000 a week or less. A fifth was taking in about $3,000 and a sixth $4,000 a week. The other six member-operated enterprises in the city included some run by the most successful members of the group and may well have been larger, perhaps averaging $10,000 a week or even more. The twelve member-operated firms in the city may thus have been taking in bets of at least $72,000 a week.

Of the two firms owned by members operating outside the main city, one was taking in about $3,000 a week and another $10,000 a week. Thus the total amount bet weekly with member-owned firms would have been $84,000 or more, or $4.37 million a year. If net profits were 5 percent of this amount, members of the group would have been earning a total of $200,000 or so in this business.[2]

One of the nonmember-operated firms in the section of the city controlled by the group has been estimated by law enforcement officials on the basis of raid data to take in $50,000 a day, or $300,000 per week. The other employs an office staff exclusive of runners and writers (messengers and salespeople) of about sixteen, indicating that it is also fairly large. It is possible that some of the member firms are equally large, which means that the estimate of $84,000 could be off by a large multiple.[3]

There is no evidence of price competition among these firms. The section of the city controlled by the group may also be divided up geographically for purposes of gambling, as one of the capos is reported to have control over a "territory" with respect to casino-type gambling.

In addition to retail numbers firms, there is one large firm (and other smaller ones) that provides a layoff service to the firms dealing with the public. When a retail firm lays off, it turns over its receipts to the layoff firm, which in turn pays all winners. The retail firm and the layoff firm split the profits. This allows retail firms to operate without the capital reserves they would otherwise need to maintain for paying winners when a heavily bet number wins.

The large layoff firm is owned by about half the ranking members of the Benguerra family, who hold varying percentages of the shares or interest in the firm. It is thus the only instance of an illegal market enterprise that could be considered a group firm. On the death of one of the partners who held the position of capo, the individual selected to replace him as capo was made a partner in the firm. He did not have to buy his share, but would have had to provide additional capital for the firm if it became necessary. On another occasion, a partner considered selling his share in the layoff firm to another individual who was already a partner.

The actual operations of the layoff firm are carried out by employees who are members of the group or close associates; one or two of the owners oversee day-to-day operations and make policy decisions. Profits are distributed to the owners every two or three months.

The layoff firm takes business from both member and nonmember retail firms. Nonmembers seek the services of the firm when they get into financial difficulty. The firm makes a loan at "20 percent" (probably a loan on which, for every $100 loaned, a total of $120 is paid in weekly installments of $10 each for 12 weeks). The layoff firm keeps 50 percent of the firm's profit, but absorbs losses if they occur. The accounting period for determining net profit is not known; the arrangement may continue until the layoff firm has made a certain profit, after which the nonmember firm has the option of dropping the layoff service and once again backing the business itself.

Retail firms operated by members receive the layoff service at a lower price than do independents—they get a 60-40 split of profits. They also apparently have the option of laying off any particular bets they wish on any given day. This allows them to back the least risky portion of their business and lay off the riskier bets, that is, the heavy bets on a particular number. Nonmember firms must lay off all bets or none.

One of the reasons number firms get into financial difficulty is that employees cheat operators. Operators of the large layoff firm are skilled in retail as well as layoff operations, and they require firms using the layoff service to follow operating procedures that prevent cheating.

The volume of business done by the large layoff firm has been variously estimated at $5 million a year and half a million a year. Profits to owners, on the basis of one item of information, were between $85,000 and $110,000 a year in the mid-1960s. As 50 percent (at least) of the profit goes to firms using the service, total profits may have been about $200,000. This in turn suggests that the layoff firm backed bets of a total amount of $1.33 million. Of this, its total receipts would be perhaps 75 percent, since expenses are deducted for the salaries or commissions of salesmen and office personnel of the retail firm before it turns its receipts over to the layoff firm. The layoff firm pays winning bets, however, on the original amount bet (600 to 1 for most numbers and less for "cut" numbers). On average it would therefore have to pay out something less than 60 percent of the total amount bet.

Thus its receipts are .75T (where T equals total amount bet) and its payout is at most .6T, leaving about .15T as profit, half or more of which goes to the retail firm. Thus profits of $200,000 a year, if they are 15 percent of the total amount bet, imply a total of $1.33 million. This formulation does not allow for office expenses, but the payout rate of .6 is higher than actual, and office expenses are probably minor because a great deal of the bookkeeping is done by the retail firms.

The owners of the layoff firm also operate a layoff in another city where members of the group are in the numbers business. Ownership is similar but not identical, and it is not known whether the information on which the above calculations are based is for both cities or only the main city.

If the estimate of the total amount bet with member-owned retail numbers firms—$84,000 per week, or about $4.37 million per year—is correct or low, the layoff firm lays off only a portion of total bets made. There are also other layoff operations; and large retail firms frequently provide a layoff for smaller operators. Use of the large layoff firm is voluntary for members and nonmembers alike, and as many as six of the member-owned retail firms are large enough to be independent of a layoff service. Thus the minimum size of an illegal numbers operation is small enough so that several firms can operate in a market of 230,000 people—the number of residents in that section of the city controlled by the Benguerra family.

The layoff permits individuals to operate a numbers firm at the retail level without a large cash reserve. Nevertheless, entry into the business by members of the Benguerra family is controlled by the top-level members (especially the boss)—the same individuals who control the layoff firm. In the numbers industry, the group thus functions as a cartel. For the potential small operator, the denial of layoff services would be an effective barrier to entry. In the one reported instance in the data sources where a member requested permission to enter, it was refused. He was told that his capo should finance the numbers business. The individual did not attempt to set up his own firm. Had he done so, he might have been denied layoff services.

The denial of entry to some members no doubt increases profits to those who do own numbers enterprises. The group's leaders do not, however, extort from the firms that are permitted to enter. Instead, their services are provided on a voluntary basis at reasonable prices or, in the case of protection from law enforcement, at cost. Thus Schelling's concept of organized crime as monopolized extortion from those who provide illegal services to the public is not applicable to the numbers industry in this city.[4]

The large layoff firm operates with a cash reserve, according to one item of information, of about $100,000, an amount that has not increased, supposedly, since the late 1950s. Although there is some investment in working capital to pay salaries and to rent office space and equipment, the cash reserve is the largest capital requirement of the business. Reinvestment of profits would therefore enable the firm to double its size in a year. A comparable return should be earned by a large retail firm that backs its own bets. Whether profits are 50 percent of capital invested as cash reserves or 150 percent, they are too great to permit continual reinvestment. Expansion through lower prices would reduce total revenues and reduce return on investment, if demand is inelastic over the relevant price decrease (increase in payout rates).

There is no indication that the numbers lotteries operated by Benguerra family members or franchised by them are anything but fair and honest. A lottery is defined here as fair if the probability is 1/1000 that any particular number will be generated as the winning number. Fairness is thus an objective term and implies no moral judgment. (Fairness refers to lack of bias and not to whether the game is fair in the sense of

56 THE BUSINESS OF ORGANIZED CRIME

an expected return equal to the entry price, the amount bet. No gambling game, legal or illegal, can be fair in the latter sense if the operators take a portion of the amounts bet to cover costs.) Fairness requires that the method for determining the winning number generate unbiased, random numbers, and that the number not be fixed or fraudulently determined. The lottery is defined as honest if the winners are paid when they win, if they are paid the amount they expected to receive when they placed their bets, and if no attempts are made to steal their winnings or otherwise prevent them from collecting.

The winning number in the lotteries operated by the Benguerra family is determined by summing the amounts to win, place, and show for three specified races at a particular race track. Each of the three races determines one digit of the number, the digit to the left of the decimal point after the summation is made. It has been stated that this system of generating winning numbers is "theoretically unfixable and unpredictable."[5] It has also been stated that in the 1930s, Otto (Abbadabba) Berman, supposedly a mathematical wizard, could manipulate mutuel odds so that lightly played numbers won.[6] This is likely to be extraordinarily difficult. A ten-horse race has 720 possible outcomes (some of which are, of course, a great deal less likely than others). Amounts to win, place, and show for these outcomes would have to be calculated and bets made to change the odds so that no outcome (or at least no likely outcome) would result in a heavily played number when the payouts were summed. Direct methods—falsification of amounts to be paid on winning horses by the track—would require interference with the pari-mutuel totalizer, which is unlikely. Whether the pari-mutuel method generates random numbers could be determined by testing for randomness, but there is no a priori reason to believe that the numbers are not random.

Law enforcement officials whom I interviewed (not identified because doing so would identify the city) are convinced that the winning numbers in this city are not fixed. The basis for their judgments is not known, but it is probably lack of evidence to the contrary. They also have found no evidence of failure to pay winning bettors, even when numbers operations are raided. This is said to be true of all the numbers banks operating in the city, which they estimate as numbering between 25 and 40. Paying winners after a raid can be costly, because either the raiding law enforcement officials must be bribed to allow the operators to keep or copy records identifying winners, or people claiming to have bet on the winning number must be paid on the basis of their word.

An organized criminal group could establish a policy that all winning bettors will be paid, in order to avoid the costs to all numbers enterprises that could result when one of them fails to pay winning bettors: the total volume of numbers betting might decline, hurting not only the organization that fails to pay, but others as well. The costs of not paying winners are, however, apparently great enough that even independent operators find cheating winners an undesirable way to do business. Customers of a fraudulent operation may cease playing or take their bets elsewhere. Law enforcement officials may also direct more vigorous efforts toward operations known to be dishonest.

The data sources on the Benguerra family include a limited amount of information on payments for protection. Monthly four-figure payments were made during 1968–1969 to the city's policemen as protection for the numbers business. This payment was made on behalf of the member of the group who collects a percentage of total amounts bet from several other numbers firms, and may have provided protection for all of these firms. Firms not paying a percentage of their bets collected may have had other arrangements for protection. It is not clear from the information available whether the payments went to uniformed policemen, plainclothesmen, or both. Individual firms might have made some protection payments on their own, for example to the precinct police having jurisdiction in the area where the particular firm operates. About $69,000 was bet weekly, or $276,000 monthly, with member firms in the section of the city controlled by the group. The four-figure payment is about 2 percent of this amount. Protection expenses as a percentage of total amount bet would be higher, of course, if other protection payments are made.

When raids and arrests occur, additional payments are required on a case-by-case basis to reduce charges, have cases dismissed, and so forth. These arrangements are made through the boss of the Benguerra family. The individuals within the criminal justice system contacted to fix cases were, in the instances cited in the data sources, individuals who had had previous dealings with the group. Case-by-case corruption expenses are usually passed along to the individuals benefitting from the service. Although the service can be denied to individual members (the boss can decide whether or not to use his contacts in the criminal justice system), the service is "sold" to members at cost. If they are unable to pay, they are given interest-free loans with easy repayment schedules. The power to deny protection services is another means of controlling entry into the industry.

The majority of funds spent for protection prevent law enforcement action rather than ameliorate it in some way after a raid or arrest occurs. Nevertheless, being able to take effective action afterward is important; inability to obtain this type of protection would increase the costs of doing business in terms of fines and time spent in jail.

Economist Paul Rubin has suggested that certain criminal goods and services—police inaction, violence, and capital—are provided to criminals by criminal firms with some market power—thus "organized crime" firms—because they show increasing returns to scale. Police inaction is considered by Rubin to be a decreasing cost activity because an official bribed to overlook one criminal activity may be more easily bribed to overlook others.[7] There are, however, other economies of scale in buying both police inaction and corruption at other points in the criminal justice system. In corrupting prosecutors, judges, and parole officers, the small operator lacks the opportunities to corrupt and the resources of the larger group. Corruption handled centrally by the head of a large group also reduces risks to the corruptee. On one occasion, the Benguerra family sought to "fix" a problem for an independent numbers enterprise operating in its territory, but the corruptee refused: the independents were considered likely to inform other law enforcement officials about the fix.

In preventive corruption—the purchase of police inaction—risks and transactions costs are also reduced when a single payment is made on behalf of several illegal enterprises. The local police, whether the uniformed precinct police or a special plainclothes gambling or vice squad, are in the position of monopolists in providing the service of nonenforcement. It is to their advantage to act as a unit in extracting payments from the illegal enterprises operating in the areas where they have jurisdiction. It also allows them to cooperate with the criminals in making selected arrests and suppressing selected illegal gambling services. Dealing with a cartel able to establish monopoly prices should increase the policemen's "take" from corruption. Collusion with the police is thus another method by which the organized criminal group may control entry into the numbers industry, especially the entry of nonmembers.

The Benguerra family is not heavily involved in bookmaking. One of its firms involved in numbers betting—one of the smallest—also takes bets on sports, collecting about $1,500 per week; and an associate of the group is in the bookmaking business. But the majority of the city's bookmaking and sports betting is handled by another criminal group.

Casino-type gambling consists of dice games (craps) and card games, such as blackjack. It is distinguished from numbers or off-track horse betting and sports betting by the presence of the bettor at the location where the gambling event that determines whether he wins or loses takes place.

During the 1960s, members of the Benguerra family operated an average of two casino enterprises a year, each lasting from a few days to several months. Permission to operate a casino enterprise is required from the top management of the group, and on several occasions such permission has been refused. Two games operating during the 1960s closed because of fear of raids, and at least one was actually raided. Another closed because police protection could not be obtained at a sufficiently low price. No information was available on why the others closed. Casino-type gambling is thus riskier than the numbers racket, where operations are not closed down because of fear of raids.

As a generalized description, the casino takes a cut of 5 percent of the total amount bet: in some cases, around $10,000 per night. (This is in addition to the house advantage in the actual play of the games; for the bettor, such casino operations are thus less favorable than those of legal casinos.) From the $500 gross revenue, all expenses of the business—salaries for workers, police protection, a fee for the owner of the casino location—are paid. A game of this size may have five people operating the casino, meet police protection of $50 per night, and pay the location owner $50 or $100 per night. Some of the operators will receive a wage of $20 or more per night; others will receive a percentage of the gross revenues, with which they may or may not be expected to pay the wages of others employed to operate the game.

Although casino-type gambling operations are risky, they provide a temporary living for those who operate them, and it is the operators who generally instigate the establishment of a game and seek permission for it. The operators are usually lower-level members of the group; upper-level members may finance casino-type gambling, but they do not participate in the operation of the casino. When credit is extended to gamblers, it is under the control of the financiers of the game.

On one occasion, the group's management forced the closing of a casino operation run by a nonmember because he was unwilling to pay a percentage to the group and hire members of the group as workers. The group may have used the threat of violence or police action to back up its demands. In any case, it was effective. The incident is a good example of what Schelling considers the basic skills of organized criminal groups— the suppression of rival illegal gambling services through extortionate means, possibly in collusion with the police.[8]

The group's illegal gambling enterprises are not of great significance in the city's economy, although the numbers industry provides some local employment. The 230,000 residents of the section of the city controlled by the group may bet an average of a dollar or two a week on numbers with member-owned firms and independents. Most of the people employed in the industry are the street workers (writers) who collect bets; these people are neither members of the group nor close associates. If full-time employees of this type collect about $500 a week each (earning an average of $125 a week, assuming their commission is 25 percent of the amount bet), the number of writers employed would be equivalent to 460 to 920 people full-time, or possibly as much as 1 percent of the civilian labor force.

The group's illegal gambling enterprises are, however, undesirable because they are associated with extensive corruption of the local police and other public officials within and outside the criminal justice system. The harm done by corruption is especially great if accepting bribes to overlook illegal gambling leads to a general breakdown of integrity within the police force, and a willingness on the part of corruptees to overlook other types of illegal activity and assist members of the organized criminal group in other ways. Paying off the police and other criminal justice officials goes hand-in-hand with illegal gambling operations. Because a large portion of the general public, the police, and public officials do not consider gambling an activity that is in itself evil or immoral, and because many people want to gamble, it is probably impossible to eradicate gambling altogether, and with it the related corruption of the criminal justice system.

The illegal numbers industry also provides the financial resources for loansharking and possibly the organizational impetus for the continued existence of the group. It is doubtful that loansharking alone as an illegal market would result in the establishment and continuance of an organized criminal group, as the need for systematic corruption and the possibility of controlling the market are less in this industry than in illegal numbers.

The economic consequences of the illegal numbers industry are considerable for the consumer. Although the industry involves neither violence nor fraud, the prices charged by the firms in the industry are monopoly prices. The firms operated by members of the Benguerra family pay out 600 to 1 on most numbers, and 400 to 1 on "cut" numbers; but payout rates in many cities are lower. At an average payout of 500 to 1, the numbers bettor's expected loss after betting $1,000 over a period of time is $500. In other words, the house edge (or advantage) is 50 percent.* By contrast, the house edge at Nevada casinos is 5−6 percent on roulette and less than 2 percent on craps. The house edge on horses and sports betting (legal or illegal) is 15−20 percent.[9]

Where the house edge is 50 percent, the bettor can bet only $1,000 (on average) before he loses $500. Where it is 20 percent he can bet $2,500, and where it is 5 percent he can bet $10,000. As another way of looking at it, the numbers bettor loses $500 of every $1,000 he bets, whereas the bettor in a 5-percent house-edge game loses only $50.

Monopoly prices in the numbers industry are thus very costly to the consumer. Gambling losses, often viewed as an undesirable consequence of numbers lotteries, would be reduced 90 percent for any given dollar volume of betting if the house edge were 5 percent instead of 50 percent. Alternatively, the dollar volume of gambling could increase tenfold if the house edge were 5 percent without increasing absolute dollar losses.

Monopoly pricing in the numbers industry has resulted in prices

---

*To gamble is to voluntarily assume risk: instead of having a dollar with certainty, the gambler gives up his dollar in return for a chance of losing it altogether or winning some multiple of it. The house takes its cut and then redistributes, on the average, the remainder of the total amount bet to the winners. The house edge (or cut) is thus one way to measure the price gamblers pay to have their dollars redistributed. A more accurate costing of the price of a bet would be to view the price as an addition, in percentage terms, to the dollar the bettor bets to receive an expected return of a dollar. In a numbers lottery paying 800 to 1, the house cut is 20 percent; the bettor would have to bet $1.25—$1 for a chance of an expected value dollar (999 chances of a return of zero, and 1 chance in 1,000 of a return of $1,000) plus $.25 for the service. The price is 25 percent. In a lottery paying 500 to 1, the house cut is 50 percent; the bettor must bet $2: $1 for the chance of an expected value dollar plus $1 for the service. The price is 100 percent. The house cut in the two examples goes from 20 to 50 percent, but the price being charged for the service goes from 25 to 100 percent. The price being charged in a 50-percent house-cut game is thus four rather than two-and-one-half times the price being charged in a 20-percent game. In a gambling game with a house cut of 6 percent, like roulette or a numbers game that pays 940 to 1, the price is less than 6.4 percent.

higher than they would otherwise be. But even if the industry were competitive, prices would not necessarily drop as low as prices for other types of gambling, especially legal casino gambling. The reason is that the technology of the illegal industry is very simple; bets are often taken by numbers writers who contact each bettor individually, and labor costs are therefore high. A legal industry would perhaps eliminate the roving writer and sell bets only as other low-value, frequently purchased items are now sold—at newspaper and cigarette stands and through vending machines of some type, and also probably by telephone. Numbers writers and collectors (those who collect bets from the writers) together receive 30–35 percent of the total amount bet.[10] Thus payout rates cannot rise above 65 percent or so without some changes in the technology of the industry, in the direction of either greater use of capital equipment or increasing productivity of the labor used in the industry.

If the findings about the numbers industry in the city where the Benguerra family operates are characteristic of the numbers industry in most major cities in the United States, the future of the industry is probably not particularly bright. Although by 1970 the Benguerra family was not faced with the takeover of its numbers industry by other ethnic minorities, several investigators have reported that the industry in many cities is being increasingly taken over by non-Italians—Blacks, Puerto Ricans, Cubans.[11] Some of these enterprises are franchised by Italian organized criminal groups, but this situation may change as other ethnic minorities advance in local government and become better able to carry out their own corruption of the criminal justice system. The industry is thus in the process of change. In the absence of the control provided by a strong organized criminal group functioning as a cartel, the industry may become more competitive. If the newcomers are less effective in controlling entry or colluding with the police to exclude new entrants, violence among rival enterprises could result. Where a strong group is lacking, individual enterprises may also turn to fraudulent practices to increase their incomes.

Price competition is also a possibility. But the industry's major problem is that its costs are too high to make it competitive with other forms of gambling. The general impression that numbers gambling is a game primarily of the poor may thus be correct. People can bet smaller amounts of money on numbers than they can bet on the horses and sports contests, the other types of gambling that are fairly readily available without spending a day at the track or taking a trip to Las

Vegas. Legal off-track betting and state lotteries are also offering competition to the illegal numbers industry. Although culture and tradition may keep many bettors loyal to the numbers, as increasing incomes and inflation make a $2 bet more possible, the 80−85-percent payout from bookmakers is likely to attract bettors away from the numbers industry.

IV

LOANSHARKING

The second illegal market in which many members of the Benguerra family are involved is loansharking. Fewer people, members and non-members, are engaged in loansharking than in numbers gambling, and the family hierarchy exercises less control over the industry than it does over gambling.

Of some interest is the question whether the cash flow from gambling enterprises is used to finance loansharking. Seven of the fourteen retail numbers firms owned by members of the Benguerra family also engage in loansharking. Five of these firms use the same personnel to carry out both activities; in a sixth the personnel involved in the two operations overlap, but there are employees involved in one and not the other business. The owner of a seventh numbers firm also operates a loan-sharking enterprise, but as a separate operation with different employees. Seven numbers firms do not engage in loansharking; one of these left the loanshark business in the mid-1960s because it was considered too risky, and three of the others are among the smaller numbers firms.

There are also five loanshark firms owned by members of the group that do not engage in numbers gambling at the retail level. Two are firms run by older members who are in the process of cutting back on their activities; two function primarily as providers of funds to other firms, which lend on their own account and on the account of the provider, for a percentage; and one is located outside the inner-city area in which the group controls numbers gambling.

Thus several owners of large numbers firms have also entered loan-sharking, perhaps because illegal funds earned in the numbers industry cannot be profitably reinvested there, and these funds provide the owners with the capital required to enter the loanshark industry. (Loans are not, however, made to customers for the purpose of numbers gambling, which is a cash business.) The Benguerra family does not control entry into the loanshark industry, although it does control competition to some extent by specifying that only one loanshark may lend to a particular borrower. The group's loansharks seldom use violence; but the group as a whole has a reputation for the effective use of violence that can be drawn upon by members in collecting debts.

Most of the loanshark firms employ people who make loans and collect payments; they also employ, at times, collectors who are "strong men" or "muscle men." Most of these employees are members or close associates of the group, that is, category A associates. Employment is less extensive in this business than in the numbers business; there are also fewer customers.

In the data sources for this study, lending rates during the mid-1960s were quoted as 5 percent for one day, 10 percent for one week, and 20 percent for periods over one week. Another quotation stated that a ten-day loan was given at the rate of 20 percent. The predominant practice appears to be the 20-percent loan, under which the borrower repays, in equal installments, the amount of the loan plus 20 percent over a period of ten to twelve weeks. Thus the first week he would receive the principal, say $100; for each of twelve following weeks he would pay $10, which includes principal and interest. Using internal rate of return calculations, this amounts to an interest rate of approximately 150 percent a year. This is much lower than the alternative rate structure of 20-percent interest per week with lump-sum principal repayment cited by Seidl for some cities.[1] That alternative rate structure is over 1,000 percent a year.

Those who finance loansharking allow their employees to approve loans of under $200. A financier-lender who lends in amounts of $1,000 or over is considered a big loanshark, and all but one of the firms involved in loansharking is capable of lending in such amounts. A loan of $3,000 or $5,000 is considered very large. Although there are statements reported in the data sources to the effect that someone may owe a loanshark $10,000 or more, it is likely that these are business investments rather than instances of loansharking, although admittedly the distinction is hard to make.

It is difficult to estimate on the basis of available information the total amount of loans outstanding for the twelve loanshark firms owned by members of the Benguerra family. A loanshark operation not known to have been associated with the Benguerra family, run by two men in the mid-1960s, is supposed to have had $250,000 outstanding, loaned to between 250 and 300 customers. This operation was apparently a full-time job for the two operators, who collected payments themselves. Whether the Benguerra family has firms doing this volume of business is not known. A large loanshark often has several loans of $1,000 outstanding. A total of $10,000 for each of the Benguerra firms except the smallest is probably a reasonable mean figure; but some firms could be much larger. One loanshark in the family who also handles funds provided by one of the wealthier members employs one person who collects payments at a stationary location. The people who make payments could, however, be employees collecting from other borrowers rather than borrowers themselves.

In 1970 consumer credit outstanding in the United States was $126,802 million, or about $634 per person.[2] The estimated $100,000 outstanding in loans made by the group's loanshark firms is not necessarily loaned only to the approximately 230,000 residents of that section of the city controlled by the group; but even if it were, the amount is only $.43 per person, and would be only $4.30 per person if loansharks in the city have a total of $1 million in loans outstanding. Thus loansharks in this city provide well under 1 percent, and probably closer to one-tenth of 1 percent, of consumer credit in the city, or even less since some of their loans are made to businesses.

Although loansharking would be a highly profitable business if all amounts due were paid in full and on time, allowance must be made for bad debts. The use of force by members of the Benguerra family to encourage payment is almost nonexistent. On one occasion, 115 borrowers were interviewed by law enforcement officials. Only one reported having been threatened, and all denied the use of violence. There is no reason to assume that these borrowers were not telling the truth. People are often afraid to testify openly in organized crime cases, but they are frequently willing to discuss their experiences with law enforcement officials.

Because there is no legal collection procedure, who the borrowers are, why they borrow at rates so much higher than legal rates, and how they manage to repay loans are questions of more than passing interest.

A major category of customer is the gambler. Some gamblers may offer the best credit risks. No quantitative estimates can be made from the data available; but some loans are made to men with good reputations in the community who have incurred sizable debts in illegal gambling. It is possible that at least some of them have the resources—stocks and bonds, for example—to pay their debts; they borrow when and where they incur the gambling debt, or shortly thereafter, repaying as they liquidate their investments.

A second category of borrower is the owner of a small business. One of the firms engaged in loansharking is concerned heavily with lending to owners of businesses at which the vending machines of the firm belonging to the loanshark are placed; thus the loansharking business is closely related to the legitimate business operation. Loans are then paid from proceeds of the vending machines. Some of these loans are made interest-free in order to obtain the location for the vending service. Such loans are risky to the extent that the legitimate business may fail before the loan is paid; because of this such loans were cut back in amount and number at times during the 1960s. Loans are also made to other small businessmen.

Another category of borrower consists of associates in illegal gambling activities. If the gambling business operated by the borrower is profitable, it is reasonable that such a loan will be paid; if not, members of the group are in a position to take over the gambling business itself.

In the early 1960s loans were made by one or more loansharks to many employees of one particular business, apparently for personal expenditures. A considerable number of loans have also been made by members of the Benguerra family and independent loanshark operations to automobile salesmen, some of whom use the loans to finance the purchase of cars for people who cannot obtain automobile financing through conventional channels. It is possible that such loans are at times for the purpose of meeting down-payments, in which case the car itself would be collateral for the legitimate loan. If there is no other loan on the car, the car can be used by the loanshark as collateral, and occasional examples of cars provided to members by borrowers in the automobile sales field occur; however, the repossession and disposal of cars in general is not mentioned in the data sources.

In his work on loansharking, John Seidl reports interviews with "unrationed" borrowers—borrowers who could, according to their own claims, borrow legitimately but preferred to borrow from loansharks for what Seidl hypothesizes to be the following reasons: secrecy, informality, speed, convenience, and availability of funds.[3] One of Seidl's unrationed borrowers borrowed from loansharks until he arranged a line of credit at a local bank. Certainly the borrower who is a sufficiently good credit risk to obtain loans through legitimate lending institutions is also a better risk for the loanshark than the rationed borrower, but it is likely that the demand for loans at interest rates of 150 percent a year by unrationed borrowers is limited—also, perhaps, inelastic at interest rates in the range of 150 percent a year. In other words, reducing the annual rate to say, 120 percent or even 100 percent a year may not result in an increase in volume great enough to keep total revenues from declining. The factor of secrecy—concealment of borrowing from family, friends, bankers, the general public—is therefore probably of primary importance.

Among rationed borrowers, loans from loansharks are, by definition, the only source of loans. The interesting question is this: how can a borrower judged too risky for a loan at legitimate rates pay a loan at 150-percent interest? It is possible that threats made by the loanshark cause the borrower to find means of payment that, had he turned to such sources before borrowing, would have made the loan unnecessary. Thus he may borrow against the cash value of his life insurance, borrow from friends and family, pawn or sell assets that he was unwilling to pawn or sell originally; or he may turn to illegal methods, such as theft or embezzlement; or he may risk having his business taken over by the lenders. In one case during the 1960s, efforts by Benguerra family loansharks to collect a loan from a small businessman became strenuous only when the man's business went into bankruptcy.

In conclusion, the demand for loans at loanshark rates is likely to be limited, and many of the loans are likely to be hard to collect. This does not, then, appear to be a business that can be expanded greatly, even if rates were lowered somewhat. The high interest rates reflect the high risk of bad debts and cannot be used as a first approximation to a rate of return on funds loaned. The 20-percent, fully amortized loan could in fact reflect a competitive market in rates for illegal loans or loans lacking legal standing, in contrast to the rates of over 1,000 percent a year charged in some cities.

Seidl's study of the criminal loanshark industry offers an analysis that may explain why rates differ so greatly in different cities. Using primarily information obtained in interviews with law enforcement officials and a few lenders and borrowers, he compares the criminal loanshark industries in New York, Detroit, Philadelphia, Cleveland, Chicago, and Boston.

He suggests that the structure of the loanshark industry in each of these cities is a function of the structure of the local underworld. The New York underworld is oligopolistic; the five oligopolists, through collusion or conscious parallelism, control the allocation of markets and enterprises among competing criminal organizations. Within each oligopolist are a number of loanshark organizations. The oligopolists lend to the loanshark organizations without strings: that is, the loanshark organization lends on its own judgment but must repay the original lender whether or not its borrowers default. Loans are made on the basis of a lump-sum repayment of principal. Prices are controlled and the use of violence in collecting debts is limited.

The Detroit underworld is described by Seidl as a cartel comprising criminal groups of different ethnic backgrounds; the cartel is controlled by the Italians. Criminal enterprises are controlled directly by the cartel or indirectly through an extortionate taxing system. The cartel allocates loanshark territories to loanshark enterprises and controls interest rates. Principal reduction requires a lump-sum payment. The cartel's distinguishing feature is that it attempts to restrict funds lent by loanshark enterprises to those funds it has supplied. All funds are therefore lent with strings; the six to ten loanshark organizations existing within the cartel are closely supervised. The use of violence is limited and controlled.

The Philadelphia and Cleveland underworlds are multiorganizational, but the Italian groups there are cartels within their own geographical areas. Loansharking, especially the large-loan business, is primarily the province of the Italian groups. The cartels do not extort from the loanshark organizations within them. Loans are repayable in equal installments that include repayment of principal. Violence is minimal.

The Boston underworld is considered by Seidl to be in transition from multiorganization to cartel, and in this process the loanshark industry has become larger and is lending on a lump-sum principal reduction basis rather than making installment loans. The Chicago underworld is classified by Seidl as a cartel; the loanshark industry is similar to that in Detroit except that violence as a collection method is much more common.

Seidl's description of organized criminal groups shows that they perform a variety of cartel or regulatory functions and offer their members the benefits of size; they have within them business firms involved in various enterprises. The group (or organization) and the firm are not synonymous. The Detroit, Chicago, and possibly Boston cartels appear to have established an extortionate claim to some portion of the revenues or profits of subsidiary enterprises. In these cities Seidl found that loansharking was highly centralized. Entry into the industry was controlled, and attempts were made to limit funds loaned to those provided by the individuals controlling the industry. In other cities this type of control did not occur, and although some individuals provided funds to be loaned by others, they lent them "without strings." In other words, the lenders at retail level made loans on their own judgment but had to repay the original lender whether or not the borrower defaulted.

The loansharking industry in the city where the Benguerra family operates (specifically, that portion of the industry for which they are responsible) is an example of the second type, where centralized control (possibly extortionate, especially from nonmember firms) is not the case. Although there are fewer loanshark firms than there are numbers firms operated by members of the group, permission from management is apparently not required to enter the business. This conclusion is based on the absence of any information in the data sources indicating that permission is required for entry. By contrast, the data sources include frequent reports that the permission of the boss is required to enter gambling and that requests for permission were turned down. There is also no indication in the sources of geographical or other restrictions on members who do enter the business. They are free to lend their own funds.

The two known cases of exit from the loanshark industry in this city also support the conclusion that there is little centralized control. In one case, the loanshark died. Other members of the Benguerra family attempted to collect the money owed him but could not do so, except for loans made to individuals who were close and continuing associates of the group. Had the loanshark been closely supervised, as is the case where control is centralized, it is likely that debts could have been collected because information on borrowers, the amount of their debts, and so forth would have been available to individuals other than the deceased loanshark. In the second case of exit, the loanshark firm decided the industry was too risky and offered to sell the business (to other members of the group, not to outsiders) for the amount of loans outstanding. The data sources provide no information on whether the owners were successful in selling the business, rather than simply dissolving it. That they could offer to sell for the amount of loans outstanding indicates that they were lending their own funds and were not franchised by a central controlling firm.

No information was available on whether loanshark firms are free to lend at rates negotiated by them with borrowers. Negotiated rates may vary more than quoted rates. Actual rates can also be influenced by the loanshark firm's policy on defaults. Cressey and Ianni report that interest rates are not fixed, but vary with economic conditions and are negotiable.[4] Cressey's statement applies to organized crime in general rather than any particular group or city. Ianni's statement concerns only the New York City group that was the subject of his study.

In spite of ease of entry, loanshark firms within the Benguerra family show no indication of competing directly with one another for the same customers on the basis of price or any other feature of the service. The data sources report no instances of a member complaining to his superiors in the group that other members were attempting to take customers or a market away from him. The judicial process does exist to handle such a situation were it to occur. Thus the industry may be competitive with respect to new customers and new markets only.

The use of violence by the Benguerra family to collect loanshark debts is infrequent. Only one case of the use of violence is known in the 1960s, although others may have occurred. The instance of threats of violence is greater, and the reputation of the group acts as an implicit threat of violence. Whether permission from the boss or other ranking members of the group is required before violence can be used is not known.

Only one loanshark at a time is supposed to lend to a customer, an arrangement that protects the loanshark's interest in the borrower's capacity to repay in the absence of legal arrangements, such as a secured interest in assets and bankruptcy laws. It was suggested earlier that one governmental function of an organized criminal group might be to establish and protect the property rights of its members in illegal market enterprises. Insofar as the group controls entry and competition among members, it is functioning as a cartel. If in addition it acted as a trustee for an illegal enterprise, if the member-owner were incarcerated or if he sold an illegal enterprise for the benefit of dependents of a deceased member, there would be support for a governmental function in protecting property rights. No instances of such a role can be inferred from information in the data sources.

On one occasion the friends of a deceased member attempted to collect loanshark debts owed him for the benefit of his widow, but were largely unable to do so. The leaders of the group were not involved in this effort. With the exception of this case, the fate of illegal market enterprises whose owners died or were incarcerated during the period of this study was not reported in the data sources. It seems likely that such enterprises are taken over, when possible, by partners or employees of the owner. It is a reasonable, if not fully supported, conclusion that the group does little to eliminate the risk of loss of the going-concern value of an illegal market enterprise in the event of the death or incarceration of the owner-member.

On another occasion reported in the sources, the group arbitrated a dispute among several loansharks who had made loans to a single individual. Some of the loansharks were members of the group and some were not. The group also provides a loosely organized credit evaluation service that covers at least some potential borrowers, perhaps as much for the purpose of determining whether they have other illegal loans outstanding as for the purpose of providing some sort of credit rating. These services are important to the individual loanshark firm, but they are not extortionist (no fees are charged), nor are they used as methods for excluding new entrants. At the same time, they mitigate against head-on competition for the same customers and markets.

As for employment in the industry, the Benguerra-associated loanshark firms are small. One or two individuals may perform all functions: providing capital, evaluating potential borrowers, and collecting payments. When as many as four individuals are involved, they are usually also active in other businesses and do not devote full-time effort to loansharking. In such a situation, two or three of the individuals are employees. In two or three cases, a financier provides funds and the business is entirely operated by another individual and a few employees. The operator also lends on his own account.[5]

In summary, numbers gambling and loansharking are the two illegal industries that generate most of the illegal income of members of the group, as members were not engaged during the 1960s in illegal drug markets and were only occasionally involved in predatory criminal activities.

The financial data on the two industries are insufficient to provide anything but rough estimates of the profits generated. The estimate of $4.37 million in total amount bet on numbers with member firms would result in profits of over $200,000 a year if profits are about 5 percent of the total amount bet. The large layoff firm's annual profits of $100,000 or so are partly attributable to the business of independents and are thus in addition to the earnings of the retail firms. Loansharking may generate another $100,000 in annual profits. These figures would be low if the volume of bets and loans is greater than the conservative estimates on which they are based.

In addition to the several hundred thousand dollars in annual profits—all in currency—fifteen members of the group earn wage income through employment in numbers gambling and loansharking. Thirteen of the group's sixteen close associates also earn income in illegal market activity, usually as employees. It was estimated that thirteen of the fifteen members employed in numbers and loansharking had incomes in 1968–1969 of $20,000 a year or less, in some cases much less. (These estimates include income from both legal and illegal sources; their derivation is explained in Chapter VI.) By contrast, of the 28 members of the group involved in ownership of illegal market enterprises, only five are estimated to have incomes of less than $20,000 a year. The 28 owners include eighteen in retail enterprises (sometimes in partnership with each other) and ten financiers or owners of wholesale enterprises such as the large layoff firm. Four of the ten are also active at the retail level.

Of the 75 members of the Benguerra family, 43 have income from illegal market enterprises; 32 members of the group and three of its close associates are unknown to have such income. Two members are in jail. Fifteen are retired and another five are in the process of retiring. Three own or manage major firms in vending, trucking, and real estate; another owns a bail bonding business making loans at loanshark rates, and two others operate a small business used as a place for other members to carry out illegal market activities.

The remaining seven individuals are neither retired, semiretired, nor in jail, but have no known involvement in criminal activity, either in illegal market enterprises or otherwise. The jobs held by six of them and the legitimate business owned and operated by the seventh are independent of illegal market enterprises. Although some of them have on occasion participated in criminal activity, they have no known active role as members of the group. Some may have left illegal activities because of lack of success, and some may have joined the group because a friend or relative encouraged them to do so; but at the time when the data were gathered, they are essentially members who would not have been identified as members except for reports by informants of membership and induction.

V

LEGITIMATE BUSINESS INVESTMENTS

The 75 members of the Benguerra family and their sixteen category A associates—that is, associates who fulfill formal requirements for membership, associate closely with at least two members of the group, and are involved in or knowledgeable about illegal activities of the group—own or have an interest in a considerable number of legitimate business enterprises. Category A associates are included in this analysis because their association with members is sufficiently close for their legitimate holdings to be integrated into the group's operations to the same extent as are those of members.

The existing literature specifically relating to the legitimate business involvements of members of organized criminal groups describes their methods of entry, exit, and operation and offers anecdotes about particular business ventures.[1] There is generally little explanation or theory beyond what can be inferred from the particular cases described. Although a few surveys of legitimate business holdings of "organized crime" have been made, they generally fail to define criteria for the selection of the organized criminals whose business investments are surveyed, or to explore the relationship between the illegal and legitimate enterprises of the subject group. (Ianni's study dealing with the core members of an organized crime family in New York City is an exception.)[2] These surveys will be considered in greater detail in Chapter VII.

Disagreement exists on the extent to which the aggressive use of illegal methods is characteristic of the legitimate business activities of organized criminal groups. The organized crime task force of the President's Commission on Law Enforcement and Criminal Justice stated that:

> Organized crime is also extensively and deeply involved in legitimate business and in labor unions. Here it employs illegitimate methods—monopolizations, terrorism, extortion, tax evasion—to drive out or control lawful ownership and leadership and to exact illegal profits from the public.[3]

Thus one view is that organized criminal activity in legitimate business is aggressive and directed toward the goal of extraordinary profits through illegal methods. Another interpretation, presented by Ianni, is that increasing investment in legitimate business is primarily an effort to become respectable. Ianni was not able to acquire in-depth data on the relationships between illegal and legitimate enterprises in the organized crime family that he studied. But he notes two significant trends: continued expansion into legitimate business and increasing separation of legitimate and illegitimate activities; the two are no longer operated from the same location by the same managers, even though there are some funds flows between them. He also states that "the movement of the younger generation of the four lineages out of the family business seems to support the thesis that for Italian-Americans, as for other ethnic groups, organized crime has been a way station on the road to ultimately respectable roles in American society."[4]

MacMichael specifically deals with the hypothesis that organized criminal involvement in legitimate business is insignificant as a threat to the legitimate business community.[5] He had planned to test this hypothesis by comparing the incidence and seriousness of illegal operation and of violations of regulations in businesses owned and controlled by members of organized criminal groups with that in legitimate businesses owned and controlled by others. But he found it impossible to gather the data necessary to test his hypothesis. One reason was that the data available from law enforcement officials did not distinguish among different types of organized criminal involvement with legitimate business. Businesses employing a member of an organized criminal group, businesses used as meeting places by members but owned by nonmembers, and businesses owned and controlled by members of organized criminal groups were all classified as "infiltrated by organized crime." A more important reason, in MacMichael's view, for the impossibility of testing his hypothesis was that legitimate businesses in which organized crime is involved are much more closely observed by law enforcement officials than other businesses. Thus the incidence of violations, even if basically the same, would appear higher for the criminal groups because violations would be more likely to be uncovered in businesses owned and operated by members of organized criminal groups. Melvin Bers, a labor economist, suggests that the attempt by those involved in illegal markets to achieve extra profits in legitimate business through unfair advantage and predatory methods is limited by the risks such techniques entail: risks of loss of legitimate sales as well as the threat to continued operations of illegal markets.[6]

Thus, different writers have reached different conclusions on the dangers of organized criminal involvement in legitimate business and on whether the aggressive use of illegal methods is characteristic of this involvement. The concern about these activities is not a generalized concern about the entry of individuals with criminal records (or even convictions related to illegal market activities such as gambling, loan-sharking, and narcotics trafficking) into legitimate business. It is instead a concern with the entry of organized criminal *groups*, with their poten-tial capability for concerted illegal action, including the use of violence, corruption, and funds obtained through illegal market enterprises.

The nature of organized criminal involvement in legitimate business and the extent to which it constitutes a threat to the legitimate pursuit of business enterprise, and the implications for public policy, cannot be resolved adequately by considering only individual examples, for anec-dotal evidence can be found to support a variety of conclusions. Further-more, as Ianni has pointed out, entry into legitimate business is not, in the group he studied, a recent phenomenon, but began when the group's illegal enterprises were first established.

The current debate on organized criminal activity in legitimate business is centered on the public-policy-oriented question of its dangers to legitimate competitors and consumers. The position that legitimate business activity is not a threat is argued primarily from the sociological perspective, on the basis that it is evidence of the desire on the part of members of organized criminal groups to assume a respectable role in American society. This view is consistent with Bell's hypothesis that organized crime is a means of social mobility in American life.[7]

But respectability is only one goal of legitimate business activity by members of organized criminal groups. There are also a number of more strictly economic reasons why members not only enter legitimate business, but enter particular kinds of legitimate businesses.

The organized criminal group is the focus of this study, and the basic hypothesis set forth here is that the legitimate business activities of an organized criminal group and its members can be explained by the group's illegal market enterprises and their organization, by the nature of the group itself, and by the position in which membership in such a group and the earning of illegal income places the individual. In other words, the purpose is to explore the extent to which organized illegal market activity generates the need for legitimate business investment and influences the economic benefits to be gained from particular types of legitimate business investment.

As has been established, the Benguerra family has within it several retail firms in numbers gambling and loansharking owned and operated by members. The group itself is not a firm. In the numbers business it functions as a cartel, restricting entry of both members and independents. Its cartel functions in loansharking are more limited. It may control the entry of independents in the section of the city where it operates, but it does not control the entry of its own members.

The group has functions, however, beyond those of a cartel; these have been described as quasi-governmental. It controls the use of violence and the distribution of protection from law enforcement. Although the group controls competition among members and protects illegal markets from independents, it does not appear to have effective arrangements for establishing and protecting property rights in these enterprises in the event of the death or incarceration of a member. Thus, there is a peculiar combination of independence of individual firms in illegal market enterprises, and of centralized control that goes beyond the cartel role but is not extensive enough to eliminate the risk of loss of assets when the owner is not there to protect them.

Second, the illegal market enterprises of the members generate a considerable illegal cash flow. I estimated from the limited information in the data sources that profits (all in currency) of at least several hundred thousand dollars are generated annually. It is unlikely that these funds can be profitably reinvested in illegal market enterprises without aggressive expansion of the territory controlled by the group. Thus some members of the group are in the position of having an "oversupply" of illegal funds, which they cannot profitably use to expand illegal gambling and loansharking in their city.

Third, profits earned in illegal enterprises formed by members of the group and their associates belong not to the group, but to the owners of the enterprises. Even if this were not the case, the organized criminal group has no legal standing as a corporation or partnership, and tax returns must be filed on behalf of an individual, a corporation, or a partnership with legal standing.

The Benguerra family is known to law enforcement officials at the local, state, and federal levels. Data sources for this study show that its members have been under investigation since at least 1961. This investigative attention is directed toward criminal activity including tax evasion identified by net worth analysis. The Intelligence Division of the Internal Revenue Service devoted considerable effort to investigating organized crime during the 1960s, and participated in the organized crime strike forces operated in several cities by the Department of Justice.[8] An analysis of federal indictments of members and associates of the Cosa Nostra shows that over 10 percent were for tax evasion.[9]

The prevention of a tax evasion charge based on a net worth analysis requires that the individual member of the group report sufficient income on his tax returns to account for overt consumption and the change in his net worth over any period of time chosen by the tax authorities (subject to a six-year statute of limitations for criminal fraud charges). A tax evasion case can be based on failure to report specific income, where the charge is supported by records that the income has been paid or received. The net worth analysis provides evidence for the receipt of income in the absence of records. The first type of charge would be more likely where legal income, rather than illegal income, is not reported.[10]

The tax evasion case based on the net worth approach thus presents problems in two areas: savings or investment and personal consumption expenditures. These problems arise to the extent that the taxpayer can be shown to have assets or to have made consumption expenditures. The individual can make consumption expenditures and hold assets of two types, hidden (or concealed) and open.

Personal consumption expenditures can be concealed by using currency to purchase items and by channeling consumption into items that can be concealed rather than those with high visibility, such as houses and automobiles. Savings and investments can, for example, be hidden in a cash hoard or an investment in real estate in someone else's name, and such assets will not enter into the net worth calculation. But income from hidden investments and proceeds from their sale present the same problem as income from an illegal market enterprise. A device such as a foreign bank account can be used to "clean" money so that its source is concealed, but such devices will not make possible open consumption, savings, and investment with these funds or the proceeds from them. The resulting investments are hidden investments as long as the individual is in the jurisdiction of United States authorities.

The illegal market activity of the members of the group and the nature of the group itself lead to a variety of reasons or objectives for entry into legitimate business. First, the individual with illegal income needs a tax cover—a source of legitimate or apparently legitimate income that can be reported on his tax returns to account for overt consumption and changes in his net worth over any period of time chosen by the tax authorities. The tax cover reduces the risk of a tax evasion charge based on the net worth approach. Second, in carrying out illegal market enterprises, many factor inputs used in the legitimate world may also be needed: transportation, warehousing, communications, raw materials, office machines and supplies, and general overhead. A front or a place to do business is the most obvious factor input for numbers enterprises and loansharking, where capital equipment requirements are minimal.

Third, legitimate businesses can be used by leaders of the group to provide services to members: jobs for parolees, jobs for members needing a real or apparent source of legitimate income, and the payment of fees to legitimatize an illegal transaction such as a bribe. Fourth, a member may seek to invest in legitimate enterprises to provide security of income and transferability of assets to dependents. He thus diversifies against the risk of losing illegal income or wealth as the result of prosecution and conviction or death, disability, or rejection by the group (withdrawal of some or all services provided to members). By doing so he protects himself and his family, not only from law enforcement but also from the group and its possible failures as a quasi-government.

Finally, profit is a possible objective. Members of organized criminal groups can be distinguished from the general population by a peculiar set of skills and resources: a capability for violence and a reputation for its effective use; experience in the corruption of public officials and an established group of corruptees; a cash-rich position, especially in illegally earned cash; skills in the evaluation of credit risks, especially borrowers whose loans will not have legal standing; and (possibly) a greater willingness than the general population to engage in criminal activity. It is possible that members of organized criminal groups are attracted to businesses in which those skills and resources can be used to advantage.

Whether there is evidence to support the hypotheses that members of organized criminal groups enter legitimate businesses for the reasons described above, and second, whether they enter particular businesses or lines of trade in which their peculiar skills and resources are especially useful, is considered in greater detail in the next chapter. Here, the legitimate business holdings of all members of the group, whether or not they are involved in illegal activity and whether or not the businesses were entered or are operated illegally, are described.

The data sources for this study made no attempt to analyze legitimate business holdings by industry, geographical location, or any other method. I have therefore classified legitimate business holdings by four-digit Standard Industrial Classification (SIC) codes. The businesses are identified by these codes and the standard list of short SIC titles.[11] The classifications are based on the names of the businesses and descriptions of the products or services sold. Where information was insufficient to classify businesses by four digits, two- or three-digit codes were used.[12]

Most of the businesses owned and operated by members of the group and their close associates are *within the city limits*. Others are outside the main city but within commuting distance (less than two hours one way). These businesses are described as located *nearby*. Some business holdings of the group are located in *distant* cities—usually in other parts of the United States but occasionally in other countries. The term distant thus identifies businesses too far from the main city to be subject to day-to-day operating control.

The data on legitimate business holdings were most complete for the 1968–1969 period, that is, the *current* period. Where businesses had been owned and operated during the 1960s but not in the 1968–1969 period, the term *former* is used. The term *possible* refers to businesses where it is not known whether ownership existing in the earlier 1960s has continued into the 1968–1969 period. It is also used, with less frequency, in cases where a member is rumored to have an interest in the business but information is insufficient (at least for the period being analyzed) to state this with certainty.

On the basis of the data sources, members of the Benguerra family and their associates were found to have current, possible, or former investments in 144 establishments, as summarized in Table 1.

TABLE 1

LEGITIMATE BUSINESS HOLDINGS OF MEMBERS OF THE
GROUP AND THEIR ASSOCIATES: SUMMARY

| | *Number of establishments* | | | |
	Within city	Nearby	Distant	Total
Current	57	27	7	91
Possible	18	10	11	39
Former	10	2	2	14
Total	85	39	20	144

For purposes of discussion, the 144 businesses have been grouped into categories as follows:

Eating and drinking places (46). With a total of 46 establishments in two industries, this is the largest number of firms in any category.

Other retail trade and services (25). Like eating and drinking places, other retail establishments can provide a tax cover and a place to carry out illegal market activities. This category includes 25 establishments in 13 different industries.

Food and kindred products: manufacturing and wholesaling (11). This category includes nine establishments (two of which are included in totals for other categories) under common ownership and management, as well as four others in the same industries. The corporation and its subsidiaries comprising the establishments under common management is the largest integrated legitimate business enterprise owned and operated by a member of the group. None of the establishments in this category is known to be a front for illegal market operations.

Construction and building services (7). Seven firms in construction or building services make up this category. These two types of establishments are discussed together because both offer the possibility of corruption of public officials in obtaining contracts. None is known to be associated with illegal market enterprises.

Miscellaneous (8). There are eight establishments in various lines of trade, including trucking, in this category.

Vending machines and related businesses (13). This category includes thirteen firms, some of them among the largest firms owned by members of the group.

Casinos and related services (12). Nine casinos and three travel agencies compose this category. The travel agencies book junkets to casinos; loans to the gamblers at loanshark rates may be approved and collected by members of the group.

Finance, insurance, and real estate (18). This category includes eighteen establishments and may be a major use of members' funds.

Miami investments (4). Members of the group have investments in ten ventures in Miami, Florida. (Six of these are included in the totals for other categories.)

Table 2 presents a comprehensive list of the establishments owned or controlled by members of the Benguerra family and their close associates. The establishments are listed by SIC code and have not been grouped into the above categories. In the following sections, the categories of legitimate business investments summarized above are discussed, as well as members' investments in stocks and bonds and property.

EATING AND DRINKING PLACES

Eating and drinking places compose the largest group of business investments as classified by the SIC codes, with 46 establishments formerly, possibly, or currently (1968–1969) controlled. Of the 46, it is likely that 33 are drinking places rather than only eating places, thus belonging in SIC code 5813 rather than 5812. These holdings are summarized in Table 3.

Of the 22 eating and drinking establishments within the city limits owned or operated by members of the group or their close associates in 1968–1969, ten were centers for gambling and loansharking; that is, they are the places where the members carried on these businesses, and they are all owner-operated. Another seven are probably also places where bets can be placed or casino-type gambling operated at times, but they are not, according to the data sources, the main business place of the owners, and some of them are run by hired managers. In three of the establishments, members of the group have invested without attempting to gain operating control. The remaining two were acquired as the result of takeovers on loanshark debts rather than through explicit investment; management control is exercised over them, but they are not gambling or loansharking fronts. All the establishments currently held and located within city limits are in that section of the city where gambling is controlled by the group.

Of the nine 1968–1969 establishments in nearby places but outside

TABLE 2

Legitimate Business Holdings of Members of the Group and Their Associates: Comprehensive List

	Within city			Nearby			Distant			Total
	Current	Possible	Former	Current	Possible	Former	Current	Possible	Former	
SIC code and short title										
1511 General building contractors				1						1
16 Heavy construction contractors	1									1
1621 Heavy construction not elsewhere classified	1									1
1731 Electrical work				1						1
20 Food and kindred products (mfg.)	4			1						5
2391 Curtains and draperies		1								1
3662 Radio and television communications equipment								1		1
4119 Local passenger transportation not elsewhere classified			1							1
42 Motor freight transportation and warehousing	1									1
4212 Local trucking, without storage	1									1
4213 Trucking, except local	1									1
4721 Arrangement of transportation	2							1		3
504 Wholesale trade: groceries and related products	3	1	1							5
5046 Fish and seafoods								1		1
5065 Electronic parts and equipment	1		1							2
5081 Commercial machines and equipment		1		2						3
5094 Tobacco and its products		1						2	1	4
54 Food stores				1	1					2
5411 Grocery stores	1	1	2							4
5431 Fruit stores and vegetable markets	2		1							3
5441 Candy, nut, and confectionery stores	1	2								3
5511 New and used car dealers				1						1
5541 Gasoline service stations						1				1
5611 Men's clothing and furnishings	2									2
5712 Furniture stores	1			1						2
5992 Florists	1									1
5812 Eating places and 5813 Drinking places	22	6	2	9	6	1				46
602 Commercial and stock savings banks and 604 Trust companies not engaged in deposit banking	1	1		1						3
612 Savings and loan associations	1									1
6145 Licensed small loan lenders	1									1
6146 Installment sales finance companies	1									1
6149 Misc. personal credit institutions			1							1

TABLE 2 (Cont.)

LEGITIMATE BUSINESS HOLDINGS OF MEMBERS OF THE GROUP
AND THEIR ASSOCIATES: COMPREHENSIVE LIST

	Within city			Nearby			Distant			Total
	Current	Possible	Former	Current	Possible	Former	Current	Possible	Former	
SIC code and short title										
6351 Surety companies				1						1
6531 Agents, brokers, and managers (real estate)	1						1			2
6552 Subdividers and developers, not elsewhere classified (real estate)			1							1
6611 Combined real estate, insurance, etc.	1						1			2
6711 Holding companies		3								3
6799 Investing institutions not elsewhere classified	1	1								2
7011 Hotels and motels				2			1	1		4
7212 Laundries, except power				1						1
7241 Barber shops	1									1
7342 Disinfecting and exterminating	1					1			1	3
7349 Misc. services to buildings	1									1
7394 Equipment rental and leasing	1			4	2					7
7512 Passenger car rental and leasing				1						1
7539 Automobile repair shops	1									1
7949 Amusement and recreation not elsewhere classified							2	7		9
Total	57	18	10	27	10	2	7	11	2	144

TABLE 3

LEGITIMATE BUSINESS HOLDINGS OF MEMBERS OF THE GROUP
AND THEIR ASSOCIATES: EATING AND DRINKING PLACES[a]

	Within city			Nearby			Distant			Total
	Current	Possible	Former	Current	Possible	Former	Current	Possible	Former	
SIC code and short title										
5212 Eating places and										
5213 Drinking places	22	6	2	9	6	1				46

[a]Drinking places are primarily engaged in retail sale of alcoholic beverages for consumption on the premises, but the sale of food may account for a substantial portion of their receipts (U.S. Bureau of the Budget, *Standard Industrial Classification Manual* [Washington, D.C.], 1967, p. 250). I estimate that 33 of the 46 establishments are drinking places.

city limits, three are owner-operated, and at all three gambling, loan-sharking, or both take place. The other establishments in this category are not owner-operated, and they appear to exist for the purpose of investment return, although gambling could take place at any of them.

Of the twelve eating and drinking places that may possibly still have been held during the 1968–1969 period, eight are investments rather than gambling fronts, although bets can be placed at two or three of them. The other four are more heavily associated with gambling and loansharking.

In addition to the establishments of members and associates, eight other restaurants or bars in the city are known to be places where gambling and loansharking take place, and there are probably a great many more. In three of these places, a member of the group manages or tends bar. Except that bets are taken or the place is used for meetings between a loanshark and his customers, there is no reason to assume that members of the group own or have any operating control over these establishments.

In summary, of the 43 eating and drinking establishments currently or possibly owned or controlled by members of the group and their associates, 24 are closely tied to illegal market enterprises; 17 of these function as a place to do business, not only as establishments where it is possible to place a bet with an employee. Nineteen are, as far as is known, held for reasons other than gambling or loansharking income.

To determine whether the city-located vending machine business owned and operated by members of the group and their associates has been a factor in the acquisition of restaurants and bars, an analysis was done of the places owned by members of the group in which cigarette machines were located for the two years for which data were available, 1963 and 1967. Other types of machines, usually amusement devices such as jukeboxes and pool tables, are handled by this firm, but cigarette machines are their major business and the only line on which data were available. In 1963, seven of the establishments in which vending machines were present were owned by members of the group. Four of them had been owned by members before a vending machine was acquired from a member-owned firm, and thus could not have been taken over through the vending machine firms. Three may have been purchased after the vending machines were installed. However, the purchasers were members of the group not associated with the vending companies, so it is likely that the purchases were independent of the restaurants' dealings with the vending firms.

In 1967, vending machines owned by the member-operated vending machine company were located in ten restaurants and bars that had been acquired by members of the group before the vending machines had been acquired. Vending machines were also located in two establishments that were later acquired by members of the group involved in the vending business. One of these appears to have been a takeover resulting from a gambling debt, the other a takeover resulting from a loan made to the owner to obtain the location for placement of a vending machine.

Of the 22 restaurants and bars for which information was available, members of the group were the original owners in only three cases. The other establishments were purchased or acquired as ongoing businesses, five involving mortgages, notes payable, or other borrowing. In only one case had the establishment been owned previously by a member of the group. Five were purchased outright for operating control. In another seven, investment return rather than operating control appears to have been the goal; sometimes outsiders became co-owners. In two cases, interest was acquired because of a debt not paid.

Also of interest are methods of exit. One of the establishments was closed (perhaps only temporarily) by a raid on its casino gambling operations. Two were sold, one burned (rumored to be a case of arson on the part of the owner), and another went bankrupt. (The number is greater than those "formerly" held because information was available on events taking place in 1970.)

In addition to the rental of vending machines, members of the Benguerra family own several businesses that sell to restaurants and bars. These include wholesale establishments in bakery products, yeast, ice, and meats and meat products and a firm in another area of food processing and distribution. There is also a supplier of bar equipment and an exterminating business. Some of these firms have customers among the member-owned restaurants and bars. Another organized criminal group in the city operates a linen supply service used by some of the eating and drinking establishments. There are no liquor distributorships.

Although members of the Benguerra family are acquainted with the officials of local restaurant and bartenders unions, these unions are not controlled by members. However, the data sources report instances in which union leaders have assisted in obtaining jobs for members and associates in return for help in winning elections.

Information that indicates size is available for very few of the 46 eating and drinking establishments. Four that were bought or sold exchanged hands at prices of under $50,000. Another four were offered, bought, or sold at higher prices. I visited or observed nine of the establishments. Five are centers for gambling or loansharking; four have luncheon counters and tables or booths or both, seating less than 50 people. Most serve inexpensive meals or short-order items.

OTHER RETAIL TRADE AND SERVICES

Like restaurants and bars, other retail outlets can serve as tax covers and places to carry out illegal market activities. Such establishments with the exception of casinos, which are discussed in a separate section, are presented in Table 4.

Of the thirteen establishments in retail trade and services within the city limits, all belong or belonged to members of the group or their

TABLE 4

LEGITIMATE BUSINESS HOLDINGS OF MEMBERS OF THE GROUP AND THEIR ASSOCIATES: OTHER RETAIL TRADE AND SERVICES

	Within city			Nearby			Distant			Total
	Current	Possible	Former	Current	Possible	Former	Current	Possible	Former	
SIC code and short title										
54 Food stores				1	1					2
5411 Grocery stores	1	1	2							4
5431 Fruit stores and vegetable markets	2		1							3
5441 Candy, nut, and confectionery stores	1	2								3
5511 New and used car dealers				1						1
5541 Gasoline service stations					1					1
5661 Men's clothing and furnishings	2									2
5712 Furniture stores	1			1						2
5992 Florists	1									1
7011 Hotels and motels				2				2[a]		2
7212 Laundries, except power					1					1
7241 Barber shops	1									1
7512 Passenger car rental and leasing				1						1
7539 Automobile repair shops	1									1
Total	10	3	3	7	2					25

[a]Not included in totals for this category; included in totals for Miami investments.

category A associates involved in gambling or loansharking; six of the ten known to be currently in business are places where bets are placed, loanshark payments collected, or bookkeeping for gambling carried out. Two were established specifically for one or more of these purposes.

My observation of four of these ten establishments, in combination with information from the data sources on volume or number of employees, revealed that eight are very small businesses; at four of these there is only the pretense of actually carrying out retail trade. The other six are active small businesses; one of them was reported to have a gross income of about $6,000 a year in the mid-1960s. These six stores are probably expected by the owners to at least supplement their illegal incomes. For only one of them, the automobile repair shop, is there no known connection with illegal market activity.

The small size of these establishments and the diversity of lines of retail trade disposes of any possibility of attempts to control the individual industries. Although one of them at times sells stolen merchandise, and one or more may sell cigarettes on which the state tax has not been paid, the potential profit of these illegal activities was not the main reason for the owners' entry into these businesses. The sale of stolen merchandise is only occasional and is usually initiated by the seller of the merchandise rather than the often reluctant retailer.

In conclusion, the retail trade and service establishments located in the city appear to have no advantages over those established by people who are not members or associates of the Benguerra family.

Of the nine enterprises located near the city, and currently or possibly in operation during the 1968–1969 period, only one is reported to be a location where illegal market activity is carried out. Five are small businesses operated by the owner or an employee who is a member of the group and possibly a part-owner; the other four are businesses in which partial or complete ownership has been acquired by members of the group with no apparent interest in operating control.

FOOD AND KINDRED PRODUCTS: MANUFACTURING AND WHOLESALING

One of the largest legitimate business enterprises owned and operated by a member of the Benguerra family is a food processing business. The business comprises several firms. It expanded considerably between 1958 and 1970, and the owners have both integrated vertically and invested in related businesses. The business now performs, under various corporations, interstate hauling, processing, and distributing. Investments have also been made in retail outlets that sell products of the manufacturing concern as well as other food products. And investment has been made in one other food processing business, in another marketing area.

This group of firms under common management operates in a regulated industry. The line of food products, thus the regulatory agency, with which these firms are concerned is not identified here, because the firms could be identified if it were. Instances of violation of standards of purity for the food products in question have occurred; the data sources report rumors that the management of the group of firms has attempted to bribe officials of the regulatory agency to overlook such violations. Failure to meet purity standards on occasion is a problem that all firms in the industry face and is not necessarily intentional; the willingness to bribe public officials, if such actually does take place, may provide a competitive advantage. The group of firms under common management has also been reported to engage in illegal pricing practices. On one occasion the managers knew of similar violations on the part of a competitor.

The available information is insufficient to determine the importance of illegal practices and possible bribery of public officials in the growth and profitability of this food processing and wholesaling business. If the industry were especially attractive to those willing to engage in illegal practices and to bribe public officials, it would be expected that other members of the group would enter, but this has not been the case. Only three other firms owned by members of the group are currently or possibly operating in the city limits; still another firm once operated in the city, but has been sold. No firms in food processing and manufacturing exist that are owned by members of the group and operate nearby. In one of the firms currently operating in the city, there is no operating control; another is very small.

The group of firms under common management and the firms in food processing and wholesaling operated by other members of the Benguerra family are summarized in Table 5. Of those under common management, three of the four manufacturing establishments (SIC code

TABLE 5

LEGITIMATE BUSINESS HOLDINGS OF MEMBERS OF THE GROUP AND
THEIR ASSOCIATES: FOOD AND KINDRED PRODUCTS—
MANUFACTURING AND WHOLESALING

	Establishments under common management (interstate)			Other establishments within city			Total
	Current	Possible	Former	Current	Possible	Former	
SIC code and short title							
20 Food and kindred products (mfg.)	4			1			5
42 Motor freight transportation and warehousing	1						1
504 Wholesale trade: groceries and related products	2			1	1	1	5
54 Food stores (retail)	1ᵃ	1ᵃ					
Total	7			2	1	1	11

[a]Not included in totals for this category; included in totals for other retail trade and services

20), the motor freight transportation establishment (SIC code 42), and the two wholesale trade establishments (SIC code 504) are organized as a parent firm with wholly-owned subsidiaries. The main company and its affiliates had a net worth in 1969 of $1−2 million, including real estate holdings.

The firms under common management are not gambling or loansharking fronts, although the member-owner at times may provide loanshark funds. The member-owner is also involved in various investments not related to these business holdings—investments undertaken with other members of the group who do have illegal sources of income. It is possible that the investments so made, while in the name of the owners of the food processing firms, are actually financed by others who have illegal sources of income and cannot openly invest their funds without instigating net worth cases by the Internal Revenue Service. The member-owner and his nonmember partners are in complete control of the enterprises, but the enterprises are used as a source of "front" money for other members of the group. The owners of this group of firms also at times place on the payroll members of the group or close associates who do not actually work for them, presumably because these individuals need to show a legitimate source of income.

CONSTRUCTION AND BUILDING SERVICES

The firms in construction and building services, none of which is known to be associated with illegal market activities, vary considerably in size. One employs about five people; another employs, on contracts that total close to $500,000 a year, 275 or more employees. The firms in this category are summarized in Table 6.

Of the six currently operating, four are located within city limits. Two of them, and possibly others, do a major portion of their work for units of local, state, or federal government under contracts won through competitive bidding. On occasion these contracts have not been renewed, sometimes because of less than satisfactory service. Five of the six are under day-to-day operating control of members of the Benguerra family or their associates; no information on operating control is available for the sixth. As they are in five different lines of trade and there is no joint ownership or management among them, they are assumed to operate independently of each other.

Although government investigators are critical of contracts given to firms known to be operated by alleged members of organized criminal groups, some of whom have criminal records, there is no indication of illegal operations such as kickbacks to government officials.

TABLE 6

LEGITIMATE BUSINESS HOLDINGS OF MEMBERS OF THE GROUP AND THEIR ASSOCIATES: CONSTRUCTION AND BUILDING SERVICES

	Within city			Nearby			Distant			Total
	Current	Possible	Former	Current	Possible	Former	Current	Possible	Former	
SIC code and short title										
1511 General building contractors				1						1
16 Heavy construction contractors	1									1
1621 Heavy construction not elsewhere classified	1									1
1731 Electrical work				1						1
7342 Disinfecting and exterminating	1					1		1[a]		2
7349 Miscellaneous services to buildings	1									1
Total	4			2		1				7

[a]Not included in totals for this category; included in totals for Miami investments.

The firm providing disinfecting and exterminating services has few, if any, customers among members of the group, although it does have some customers in common with a vending machine company operated by the group. The existence earlier of two group-controlled businesses in this field suggests that entry into the business is more than accidental. Although there is no indication of any attempt to monopolize or use force in selling the firm's services, it is likely that the other investments of the group in restaurants, bars, and vending machines have made it easier to market these services than if the manager of the business had no close contacts in these other industries. A linen supply firm operated by another organized criminal group also has customers in common with the vending and exterminating firms. Unfortunately, lists of customers of these businesses are not available for comparison.

MISCELLANEOUS

In this section, holdings summarized in Table 7 are considered.

Of the firms currently or possibly operating in the 1968–1969 period, the 2391 entry (curtains and draperies) and the 5065 entry (electronic

TABLE 7

LEGITIMATE BUSINESS HOLDINGS OF MEMBERS OF THE GROUP
AND THEIR ASSOCIATES: MISCELLANEOUS

	Within city			Nearby			Distant			Total
	Current	Possible	Former	Current	Possible	Former	Current	Possible	Former	
SIC code and short title										
2391 Curtains and draperies		1								1
3662 Radio and television communications equipment							1			1
4119 Local passenger transportation not elsewhere classified			1							1
4212 Local trucking, without storage				1						1
4213 Trucking, except local	1									1
5065 Electronic parts and equipment	1	1								2
5081 Commercial machines and equipment		1								1
Total	2	2	2	1			1			8

parts and equipment) are small businesses operated by the owners or a close associate of the owners. The 5081 entry (commercial machines and equipment) is one of three firms falling into this SIC code, but unlike the others (discussed later) it is engaged in restaurant and bar equipment rather than vending machines and is not known to be controlled by the member-owner. The nonlocal trucking firm is operated by a category A associate but controlled by members of the group and may be involved in stolen merchandise. No relationship to the local trucking firm or the 42 entry involved in food hauling (discussed above) exists.

No information in the data sources suggests that any of the firms in this miscellaneous category is either a front for gambling or a loansharking cover. However, the nonlocal trucking firm has at times carried on its payroll members of the group who do not work there on a regular basis. The group does not control the labor union involved, although it has made attempts to gain control.

The only firm likely to be fairly large is the nonlocal trucking firm, but unfortunately no indications of its size were available in the data sources except that a former partnership interest, percentage unknown, was for sale at one time at a price of $50,000.

VENDING MACHINES AND RELATED BUSINESSES

The members of the group own or control, or have invested in, a total of thirteen firms in the business of selling, renting, or servicing vending machines, as summarized in Table 8.

These firms vary considerably in size. One that sells tobacco products (SIC code 5094) was sold for a total of almost half a million dollars, of which Benguerra family members received one-third for their interest in the firm. Of those renting equipment, one had, in the mid-1960s, less than fifteen machines. A larger firm had over 200 cigarette machines and close to 100 jukeboxes in place in various establishments. The firms that rent machines also, at times, rent candy machines, pool tables, and pinball machines. Another still larger firm had 300 cigarette machines and 150 candy machines, did a volume of $200,000 a year, had a net worth of $54,000, and was sold by one member of the group and his associates to another member for $90,000.

The only firm for which information is available on relations with other group holdings and on economic influence in general is the

TABLE 8

LEGITIMATE BUSINESS HOLDINGS OF MEMBERS OF
THE GROUP AND THEIR ASSOCIATES: VENDING
MACHINES AND RELATED BUSINESSES

	Within city			Nearby			Distant			Total
	Current	Possible	Former	Current	Possible	Former	Current	Possible	Former	
SIC code and short title										
5094 Tobacco and its products (wholesale)[a]		1					2	1		4
7394 Equipment rental and leasing	1			4	2					7
5081 Commercial machines and equipment				2						2
Total	1	1		6	2		2	1		13

[a]Some of these firms may be or have been in the business of renting vending machines (SIC code 7394).

equipment rental firm (SIC code 7394) operating within the city. The analysis shows, for one recent year, the number of cigarette machines in place by type of establishment and location in the city (Table 9). The city has been divided into three areas, the central business district bordering the controlled section; the controlled section (population about 230,000), where the group controls gambling and where the overwhelming majority of member-owner businesses are located, including all but a few of its restaurants and bars; and other portions of the city. There is also an unknown category for machines, the location of which could not be identified.

TABLE 9

LOCATION OF CIGARETTE MACHINES OF A MEMBER-OWNED
VENDING MACHINE RENTAL FIRM

	Area of the city				
Type of location	Central business district	Controlled section	Other	Unknown	Total
Restaurant/bar	8	28	19	5	60
Restaurant/luncheonette	2	34	16	1	53
Other retail trade	2	24	14	7	47
Other	8	6	29	1	44
Unknown	—	9	10	2	21
Total	20	101	88	16	225

Almost half the firm's locations are in the section of the city where the group operates. The remainder are elsewhere, presumably almost wholly in establishments not owned or controlled by members of the group. Of those locations within the controlled section, my review of names and locations identified only thirteen owned or controlled by members of the group. Two of these are controlled because of having been taken over, perhaps through failure to pay a loan from the vending machine rental firm. Businesses owned by members of the group constitute less than 10 percent of the business of the vending company and thus cannot be considered a captive market. The placing of machines elsewhere in the city suggests that the firm is competing with other firms in the city for business.

The vending machine rental business is highly competitive. The company buys cigarette vending machines for several hundred dollars, usually in cash, although it may borrow from other sources to buy them. They must then be placed. The location owner receives $.03 per pack of cigarettes sold and does not have to pay to have the machine on location; instead, the location owner, especially the owner of a restaurant or bar, often expects to receive an interest-free loan of $500 to $10,000 from the firm that places the machine. (Actual loans are often under $1,000 and may be as low as $200.) This loan is then paid by the proceeds of the vending machines; at 500 packs per week, such a loan would be paid at the rate of $15 per week, or $780 per year.

To obtain locations, the firm operating within the city also arranges loans (and sometimes co-signs the loan papers) from two legitimate lending institutions in the city over which members have control. During the late 1960s, the firm found this to be a risky policy, as the locations sometimes went out of business before the loans were paid.

The availability of cash to lend interest-free to location owners appears to be an important factor in competition in the vending machine rental business, and the relationship between vending and the illegal cash flows generated in gambling may be an important element in making the vending business attractive for members of organized criminal groups. A second element is the relationship of the vending business with restaurants and bars. A great many members of the group have experience in operating or managing such establishments and therefore have the skills needed to evaluate the risk of loans to location owners and to take over an establishment when such loans cannot be paid.

The possibility of selling cigarettes on which state taxes have not been paid is another element of the business that may make it attractive to those willing to engage in illegal activity. But the firms considered here were established before the sharp differentials in state taxes occurred.[13] Although this activity can provide extraordinary and unexpected profits, that fact cannot be considered the reason for a decision to enter the business.

The sellers of vending machines sell not only to those who rent and service them, but also to establishments such as gambling casinos located in other countries.

CASINOS AND RELATED SERVICES

Members of the Benguerra family have at times allegedly invested in casinos located in places where casino gambling is legal: Las Vegas, the Caribbean, London, for example. They have invested, or considered investing, in at least nine such casinos during the 1960s, sometimes in amounts of hundreds of thousands of dollars. These are usually hidden investments because the various jurisdictions may have regulations forbidding investment by nonresidents (as does Nevada) or by people judged not to be of good character.

In addition to its investments in gambling, the group has controlling interest in, or close association with, three firms falling under SIC code 4721, arrangement of transportation. These firms are travel agents who book junkets to casinos in a variety of locations. The specific arrangements made with customers are not known; but in general, air and ground transportation, lodging, and meals can be arranged for gamblers at rates often below what they would have to pay if they made the arrangements individually. The casino involved may also provide each junketeer with "free" chips—chips that can be used for gambling but not exchanged for cash (although winnings may be so exchanged).

As described thus far, these junkets are legal. They may increase the revenues of the casino involved in comparison to other casinos, and perhaps they increase the total volume of casino gambling. However, another feature of the junkets, specifically those operated by the travel agencies with which members of the group are associated, is the extension of credit to the gamblers. Gambling debts usually do not have legal standing, and the provision of credit to gamblers whom the casino does not know—who may live in other parts of the country or abroad—

can be assumed to be a problem for the casino. The extension of credit by the casino is therefore guaranteed by the travel agent and his associates, making it possible for debts to be collected by people living in the same city as the gambler. The decision to extend credit is probably made by those guaranteeing payment: the travel agents and their associates, who may be members of the group. At times the casino apparently receives a percentage of debts actually collected, thus sharing with the travel agent and his associates the risk of extending credit.

Table 10 summarizes holdings in casinos and travel agencies. Two of the casinos in which members may have an interest may also have purchased vending machines from the group-controlled vending machine sales companies.

Such information as exists indicates that the members of the Benguerra family invest in casinos at times with members of other organized criminal groups, and that members of these groups are invited to participate in the financing of a casino, which may require total investments of, for example, $1.5 million. At other times, a single organized criminal group may invest with associates who are not members of another organized criminal group, in amounts of perhaps several hundred thousand dollars. Travel agencies may be the conduits for obtaining interest in casinos by members of the group.

Thus casino investment is probably a major use of funds for members of the group. When the group is invited to participate in a venture in which other groups are participating, the boss apparently has the option of going to other members of his group and inviting them to invest, at his own discretion.

TABLE 10

LEGITIMATE BUSINESS HOLDINGS OF MEMBERS OF THE GROUP
AND THEIR ASSOCIATES: CASINOS AND TRAVEL AGENCIES

	Within city			Nearby	Distant			Total
	Current	Possible	Former		Current	Possible	Former	
SIC code and short title								
4721 Arrangement of transportation	2				1			3
7949 Amusement and recreation not elsewhere classified						2	7	9
Total	2					3	7	12

Investment in casinos is long term. Junkets bring a more immediate return from the collection of loans extended to junketeers. Although the possibility of skimming—not reporting revenues—is often considered a reason for the attractiveness of casinos to members of organized criminal groups, the extension of credit to gamblers is an important aspect of casino operation and one in which members of organized criminal groups are skilled. Tax evasion through not reporting revenues is, however, more profitable in casinos than in most other businesses where skimming is possible, because taxes on total amounts bet as well as income taxes can be evaded. The members of the Benguerra group are, according to reports in the data sources, in favor of the legalization of casino gambling in areas near their city; indeed, they are enthusiastic about it. Members have made or considered business investments in a nearby area where legalization of casino gambling has been considered.

FINANCE, INSURANCE, AND REAL ESTATE

Members of the group have investments in finance, insurance, and real estate as shown in Table 11.

The banking institutions (those in SIC codes 602 and 604) are banks in which members of the group have or are rumored to have investments or board membership. In one of them, a member of the Benguerra family is the second largest shareholder but presumably exercises no control. Individual members are known to borrow from the bank within the city, which employs a relative of a member as a teller; but members also borrow from other banks and have deposits at various banks in the city. No further information is available on the types of services these banks provide to members of the group.

The savings and loan association was started by members of the group through the purchase of a dormant savings and loan charter. The personal credit institutions (SIC codes 6145, 6146, and 6149), both those currently operating and possibly the one no longer in business, make loans to customers of a member-owned vending machine company on the company's recommendation and sometimes co-signature. One of these firms is legally limited to making loans of $3,500 or less; the other can lend in larger amounts. A third business, listed under SIC code 6611 because its activities are unknown, is also associated with the vending

TABLE 11

LEGITIMATE BUSINESS HOLDINGS OF MEMBERS OF THE GROUP AND THEIR
ASSOCIATES: FINANCE, INSURANCE, AND REAL ESTATE

	Within city			Nearby			*Distant*			*Total*
	Current	Possible	Former	Current	Possible	Former	Current	Possible	Former	
SIC code and short title										
602 Commercial and stock savings banks and										
604 Trust companies not engaged in deposit banking	1	1		1						3
612 Savings and loan associations	1									1
6145 Licensed small loan lenders	1									1
6146 Installment sales finance companies	1									1
6149 Miscellaneous personal credit institutions			1							1
6351 Surety companies					1					1
6531 Agents, brokers, and managers (real estate)	1						1			2
6552 Subdividers and developers (real estate) not elsewhere classified			1							1
6611 Combined real estate, insurance, etc.	1						1			2
6711 Holding companies		3								3
6799 Investing institutions not elsewhere classified	1	1								2
Total	7	5	2	2			2			18

machine rental business. The surety company is in the bail bonding
business; informants report that the owner makes related loans at
loanshark rates.

Other institutions located in the city include two in real estate (SIC
code 6531) and five current or possible holding companies and investing
institutions. One of these firms is actively engaged in evaluating real
estate, financing real estate ventures, and lending or arranging mortgage money on residential property for members of the group and their
associates. It obtains a finder's fee when money is raised from other
lending institutions.

The real estate firm no longer in business (SIC code 6552) was a
syndicate formed for a particular venture of about $200,000; in connec-
tion with the project, changes in zoning regulations were arranged.

The three holding companies, all in the field of real estate, were active in the early to mid 1960s, but whether they are still active is not known. Some measure of control of these companies is likely, since they were managed by business associates of the group. The third was the parent company of three firms in different industries. These firms have not been included elsewhere in the analysis because there appears to be no association with members of the group, and their percentage interest is unknown.

The two investing institutions are involved in land. One is a corporation established to undertake a specific venture in the Miami, Florida, area. Another is a firm in which members of the group invested a small amount of money with many other people. In both cases, the investments are located outside the group's state.

The two firms in distant locations are in Miami, and they have some management and investors in common. One of them purchased a mortgage on a building in still a third part of the country for about $15 million. Members of the group who have invested in these firms have control to the extent that they select some of the top management.

MIAMI INVESTMENTS

Members of the Benguerra family own or have invested in several businesses in Miami, Florida.[14] Some of these have been included under other categories as distant investments. The others are summarized in Table 12.

The investments include one firm in the wholesale distribution of fish and seafoods, two hotels, and one firm in the disinfecting and exterminating field (sold before the current period) that served hotels and

TABLE 12

LEGITIMATE BUSINESS HOLDINGS OF MEMBERS OF THE GROUP
AND THEIR ASSOCIATES: MIAMI, FLORIDA, INVESTMENTS[a]

SIC code and short title	Current	Possible	Former	Total
5046 Fish and seafoods		1		1
7342 Disinfecting and exterminating			1	1
7011 Hotels and motels	1	1		2
Total	1	2	1	4

[a]Further investments in the Miami area include three firms involved in real estate and three in cigarette vending or distribution.

motels. The hotel investments amounted to over $200,000—possibly considerably over.

In addition to these investments, three firms in the Miami area in cigarette vending machine or servicing businesses (one of which has definitely been sold) were mentioned earlier. Two real estate firms controlled by members of the group also operate there, as well as the investing institution that is classified as within the group's city limits but was established to undertake a specific real estate venture in the Miami area.

STOCKS AND BONDS

Some members of the Benguerra family, especially retired members, are known to visit offices of stockbrokers or to have holdings in stocks and bonds. One of the wealthier members has stocks of four different companies; market values of three of them totalled under $6,000 as of 1969. Stock holdings of members include, among others, shares in a large bank. The shares have a market value of a few thousand dollars. Investments of this magnitude are insufficient to suggest operating control, and such investments are not listed as firms that members of the group may own or control.

Thus stock holdings of members of the group, insofar as information about such holdings is available, are minor. Savings accounts and United States savings bonds, providing greater liquidity and protection of principal, are apparently preferred to stocks and bonds of American corporations.

PROPERTY

The term property is used here to distinguish certain holdings from larger investments in real estate ventures. It is estimated that members of the Benguerra family, as individuals, own about 30 rental properties exclusive of their legitimate businesses and their own residences. These range in appraised value from a few thousand dollars to $50,000 or so, and they return modest rental incomes. Some of the properties are residential; others are buildings renting to small businesses. The businesses of the renters have not been included in the analysis, as there is no indication that they are controlled by those who own the property; nor is takeover of a business for failure to pay rent an apparent method of entry into legitimate business.

Where one of the legitimate businesses owned by a member of the group holds property carried on the books of the firm, those properties are not included in the estimated 30 rental properties here.

VI

REASONS FOR LEGITIMATE INVESTMENT

In the area of legitimate business, the hierarchy of the Benguerra family functions neither as a firm nor as a cartel. Members and associates of the group are free to enter legitimate businesses of their choice with partners of their choice, whether or not the partners are members of the group. The legitimate business activities of members are generally not predatory. The use of violence in legitimate business is minimal, a finding consistent with the limited use of violence in illegal activity and with the observation that the pattern of legitimate business investment does not reveal extortion, criminal monopolization of any industry, or the control of labor unions.

Aggressive effort to earn extraordinary profit in business or industries through illegal means does not explain the entry of members of the Benguerra family into legitimate business. Neither, however, is a desire to become respectable a satisfactory explanation. It was suggested in the last chapter that members of organized criminal groups may enter legitimate business for five reasons: to establish a tax cover; to support illegal market enterprises; to provide services to members of the group; to diversify against the risks of illegal market enterprises; and for profit. The available evidence for the extent to which each of these reasons explains the legitimate business investments of the Benguerra family is considered here.

ESTABLISHMENT OF A TAX COVER

Reducing the risk of a tax evasion charge based on the net worth approach discussed earlier is perhaps one of the primary reasons for legitimate business activity by members of organized criminal groups: if they earn illegal income, they need a source of legitimate or apparently legitimate income to serve as a tax cover. As Angelo Bruno, boss of the Italian organized criminal group in Philadelphia, was overheard to say, "I got problems because I need show money, money I can account for because when Uncle Sam comes in, you got troubles."[1] The amount of income an individual needs to report on tax returns is a function of the amount of aftertax income he wishes to openly invest and openly consume. This amount may be an increasing function of wealth and income: as wealth and income increase, so might the absolute amount of open consumption and investment. Thus, as illegal income increases, so will the size of the required tax cover. The need for a tax cover should be a sufficiently compelling reason for virtually all members of a group earning illegal income to move into legitimate business if law enforcement officials are active in bringing tax evasion charges against members of such a group.

Individuals with low illegal incomes (for example, some employees of illegal market enterprises) might satisfy the need for legitimate income with a legitimate or apparently legitimate job. Those with higher illegal incomes can be expected to have a flexible source of income, that is, one where greater than actual earnings can be reported: for example, ownership of a business in which most of the revenues are in the form of currency and there is no precise linear relationship between input or output and revenues, making it difficult for tax authorities to verify revenues and expenditures and thus profits. Moreover, as part of its function of protecting members from law enforcement activity, a group may have some means of legitimizing income or funds flows for its members.

To determine whether the objective of establishing a tax cover is a reason for the legitimate business activity of the Benguerra family, it was necessary first to identify those members considered to need a tax cover—that is, those with income from illegal market enterprises—and then to consider not only whether they do have legitimate or apparently legitimate sources of income, but also whether the legitimate sources increase in size and flexibility as illegal sources of income increase.

Of the 75 members of the group, 43 are known to have income from illegal market enterprises. (Thirty-two members and three category A associates have no known income from illegal market enterprises and thus no need for a tax cover.) In all but one case these individuals are employees, owner-operators, or financiers of gambling and loansharking enterprises; the other individual is involved in fencing stolen merchandise. Of the 43, fifteen are employees of illegal market enterprises; eighteen are owner-operators of retail illegal enterprises (sometimes in partnership with one another); and ten are financiers of illegal enterprises or owners of wholesale enterprises such as the large numbers layoff firm. Four of the ten are also active at the retail level.

All but three of the 43 group members with illegal market income also have legitimate sources of income.

To determine whether legitimate sources of income increase in size and flexibility as illegal market income increases, the amount of legitimate income should ideally be compared to the amount of illegal income. But the financial data on illegal enterprises were fragmentary, and they usually concerned total amounts bet with an illegal numbers enterprise or amounts loaned by loanshark enterprises. Moreover, data were rarely available on the wage income paid to employees of such enterprises or the income of proprietors or partners.

Although the data were too fragmentary to develop estimates of the illegal market income of each individual, it was possible to develop estimates of the total income or wealth of individual members from a variety of indicators of their financial circumstances. These indicators included, for some members, reasonably precise financial data on illegal income, legitimate income, or net worth. At times it was necessary to use less precise indicators such as the ability to make large investments, the need to borrow, information on consumption expenditures, and comments from informants on the success and financial reputation of members. Some of these indicators are relative: the need for financial assistance or the ability to invest large sums is dependent not only on income and wealth, but also on the financial responsibilities and expenditure patterns of particular individuals.

On the basis of the various indicators, members were assigned to one of the following income-wealth classes:

Low. Members with wage income of less than $5,000 a year or unemployed and willing to accept less than this amount in the absence of other income. Also, members described as "starving," "always broke," or "living off friends," and members obtaining financial support from other members.

Low to moderate. Members with an estimated income of $5,000-10,000 a year or described, for example, as "not doing too well but not starving."

Moderate. Members with an estimated income of $10,000-20,000 a year.

Moderate to high. Members with an estimated income of $20,000-30,000 a year or considered successful in legal or illegal enterprises.

High. Members with an estimated income of over $30,000 a year, in several cases $50,000-100,000 or possibly more. Indicators of the high-income high-wealth individuals include ability to invest $10,000 or more in a venture such as a casino, net worth of several hundred thousand dollars, high consumption expenditures (for example, for housing or furnishings), extensive hidden or open legitimate business holdings, reports that the individual is wealthy or very wealthy, and a reputation as very successful currently and in the past.

I am reasonably confident that members assigned to the low and high income-wealth classes belong there. There is a possibility that those in the three middle classes belong in a higher or lower one. Although the classification procedure considered both legal and illegal income, I estimated that illegal income is or has been a significant source of income for all but one of the thirteen individuals in the moderate-to-high income-wealth class and all but one of the eleven in the high class. In the three lower classes, the main source of income for five of the nineteen is legitimate employment or self-employment.

The assignment of individuals to income-wealth classes is shown in Table 13. Only twelve members of the group are estimated to have achieved an annual income of over $30,000 a year or a net worth of several hundred thousand dollars. Almost as many members have an income of less than $5,000 a year. Of the 75 members, only 26 (35 percent) have an estimated income of $20,000 a year or more.

Estimated average incomes for active members—those neither in jail nor retired—in each age group were computed by using $4,000 as the average for the low income-wealth class, $50,000 for the high income-wealth class, and mid-points of the ranges for the other three classes. The results are shown in Table 14. Average income increases with age,

TABLE 13

AGE AND INCOME-WEALTH CLASS FOR MEMBERS OF THE GROUP

| Age group | Income-wealth classes: number of members | | | | | |
	Low	Low to moderate	Moderate	Moderate to high	High	Total
35-44 years	1	3	2	1	1	8
45-54 years		3	7	2	2	14
55-64 years	7	2	5	5	6	25
65-74 years	2	1	7	3	3	16
75 and over			5	2		7
Unknown	1		3	1		5
Total	11	9	29	14	12	75

reaching its maximum for those 65–74 years of age; it then declines for those 75 and over.

The total annual income for active members was estimated at $1.2 million. As this amount includes income from legitimate business investments, legitimate employment, and employment in illegal enterprises as well as illegal profits, it is consistent with earlier estimates that the illegal market enterprises of the group may generate total profits (and also cash flow) of several hundred thousand dollars a year.

The sources of legitimate income for the 43 members of the group with income from illegal market enterprises are shown in Table 15. The three individuals for whom there is no known source of legitimate income are in the low and low-to-moderate income-wealth classes, and their need for legitimate income as a tax cover is thus minor. Of the nine employed individuals, only two have jobs that are clearly independent

TABLE 14

AGE AND INCOME OF THE 58 ACTIVE[a] MEMBERS OF THE GROUP

Age group	Number of active members	Estimated average income
35-44 years	8	$16,400
45-54 years	14	19,800
55-64 years	21	24,400
65-74 years	8	29,600
75 and over	3	21,700
Unknown	4	23,800
Total	58	

[a]Neither in jail nor retired.

TABLE 15

INCOME-WEALTH CLASS AND SOURCE OF LEGITIMATE INCOME
FOR THE 43 MEMBERS OF THE GROUP WHO HAVE
INCOME FROM ILLEGAL ENTERPRISES

		Source of legitimate income: number of members			
Income-wealth class	None known	Employment	Ownership of small business	Ownership of larger legitimate holdings	Total
Low	1	2	1		4
Low to moderate	2	3	2		7
Moderate		3	5		8
Moderate to high		1[a]	6	6	13
High			4	7	11
Total	3	9	18	13	43

[a]This individual is on the payroll of a member-owned firm but does no work for the firm. This is his only known source of (apparently) legitimate income.

of the activities of members of the group. The others are employed in fronts where they carry out their illegal activities, or they hold jobs in legitimate businesses owned by other members or arranged for them. One of them is on the payroll of a member-owned firm but does no actual work for the firm.

As Table 15 shows, as income increases there is a shift from wage-earning to ownership of a small business as the source of legitimate income. As income increases still further, there is a shift from ownership of a small business to more extensive legitimate business holdings and thus to larger and more flexible sources of legitimate income. Of the members in the moderate-to-high and high income-wealth classes, only one receives wage income, and he does not actually perform the job for which he is paid.

Four individuals in the high income-wealth class have minimal open legitimate investments, although one also has wage income that is only apparently legitimate. Three of them own retail establishments, but the amount of legitimate income that can be reported for tax purposes through these establishments is probably limited by their small size. Instead of open investment, these individuals have made hidden investments (for example, in casinos), and their open consumption is modest.

The small legitimate businesses owned and operated by members of the group involved in illegal market enterprises are, with few exceptions, businesses in which greater income than that actually earned can be reported. Most larger legitimate business holdings include such enterprises.

In addition to members of the group employed in illegal market enterprises, thirteen of the group's sixteen category A associates are also so employed. (The other three are not involved in illegal market enterprises.) With one exception all thirteen are estimated to be of moderate income, but the amount of information in the data sources is minimal. Three are known to have jobs, all in member-owned legitimate businesses. Another three own and operate legitimate businesses used as meeting places or places where illegal activities take place. No information was available on sources of legitimate income for the remaining seven.

Finally, there are three legitimate businesses owned by leaders of the Benguerra family that are occasionally used to provide members with an apparently legitimate source of income. During the 1960s, several members were on the payrolls of these firms even though they did no actual work for them. These businesses also provide actual jobs to members in need.

SUPPORT FOR ILLEGAL MARKET ENTERPRISES

The main support needed for retail numbers and loansharking enterprises is a front or place to do business, ideally a retail establishment where the owners and operators of an illegal enterprise can be reached by customers and employees. Members of the Benguerra family have seventeen proprietorships or partnerships in illegal markets. Their owners can be expected to establish fronts: seven operate retail numbers enterprises, three operate retail loanshark enterprises, and seven operate both.

Of the seventeen members involved in the proprietorships or parnerships, eleven are known to operate one or more establishments suitable as fronts. Most of these are restaurants or bars; a few are in other retail lines such as food or clothing. Two of the seventeen use establishments by arrangement with their owners; in one case the owner of the illegal enterprise apparently helped the legitimate owner establish the business to serve as a front. Three owners of small numbers businesses and one of a larger operation were not known to own or have access to any legitimate business suitable as a front, but one of them was seeking such a business.

Another approach to the question of the use of legitimate business as support for illegal market enterprises is to consider the number of establishments in retail trade or services that are owned by members of the group or their category A associates in which activity related to illegal market enterprises, including bookmaking, is carried out. No illegal market activities were reported to occur in establishments in industry groups other than retail trade and services. The data are presented in Table 16.

As Table 16 shows, illegal market activities are carried out at almost half of the group's retail trade and service establishments. Many of the 31—at least seventeen of the eating and drinking establishments and all seven of the others—function as fronts or places to do business and not only as establishments where it is possible to place a bet with an employee. Only six of the 65 retail trade and service establishments are owned by members of the group who do not have illegal market income.

The bias in the data is such that there are probably other locations not noted in the sources where the owners and employees of illegal market enterprises carry out some of the procedures involved in those enterprises. Bets on numbers are placed with numbers writers who have a route or operate out of store fronts, not at enterprises functioning as places to do business for the owners. Also, the daily accounting and banking operations of a numbers or loanshark enterprise may take place in a residence or possibly in the offices of a business not engaged in retail trade or services. Although this type of office work is carried out at some of the establishments considered fronts or places to do business, in many cases the front is the location where access to the owner or to the employees to whom he delegates responsibility is possible.

TABLE 16

LEGITIMATE BUSINESS ESTABLISHMENTS OF THE GROUP
AND ILLEGAL MARKET ACTIVITY

Industry	Presence of illegal market activity	No known illegal market activity	Total
Eating and drinking establishments	24	19	43
Other retail trade and services	7	15	22
Total	31	34	65

Thus another reason members of the organized criminal group enter legitimate business—especially retail trade and services—is to establish a front or place to do business. Almost half the currently held retail trade and service establishments of the group are associated with illegal market activities; the other half are apparently not, indicating that the need for a front is not the only reason for their ownership.

PROVISION OF SERVICES TO MEMBERS OF THE GROUP

Providing services to members is one aspect of legitimate business ownership that is covered by businesses established for other purposes. Since leaders of the group provide these services, their legitimate businesses are the ones likely to be so used.

Providing a member with a tax cover is one service of some legitimate businesses. At other times, jobs are found for members in such businesses because they need the wages and are perhaps too unreliable to work in illegal market enterprises or in fronts for them.

Three legitimate businesses that carry members on the payroll or provide jobs for members in need, in three different industries, were identified: one is a nonlocal trucking firm, one is in food manufacturing, and one is in the rental and servicing of vending machines. These are among the largest firms owned by members of the group. They are independent of one another and are owned and controlled by three different group leaders, but the leaders cooperate in finding jobs or apparent jobs for members when the boss decides that this service should be provided.

DIVERSIFICATION

The objectives of legitimate business investment already discussed are closely related to illegal market enterprises, and as a class they can be viewed as efforts to reduce the risk of prosecution and conviction for illegal activities and the failure to report income earned thereby. The legitimate businesses operated for these reasons need not be profitable in themselves to fulfill their function.

When diversification is the reason for legitimate investment, profitability and risk avoidance are important considerations, because the purpose is to provide security of income (or less variability in income) and transferability of assets to dependents. The extent to which members of a group seek legitimate investments to protect against the risks of illegal enterprise is likely to vary among groups. It may be greatest where the group is least able to protect markets from competition from outsiders or other members and least effective in corrupting public officials and thus protecting members and markets from law enforcement; where the group performs few if any welfare functions, such as ensuring jobs for members and providing retirement income, and fails to protect members' property rights in illegal enterprises on death, illness, or incarceration; and where the group is internally unstable, so that leadership succession is uncertain. The study of the Benguerra family's illegal enterprises has not shown it effective in protecting property rights in such businesses on the death or incarceration of a member-owner.

The benefits of diversification are more likely to be achieved through open rather than hidden investment because open investment offers the fullest legal protection. Although expected profitability is a requirement, the rate of return need not be as high as that on investment in illegal market enterprises. Diversification can be expected to increase with both the income and the age of the member. Legitimate business activity that satisfies the need for a tax cover may also meet the need for diversification; but a business used as a front does not because a raid by law enforcement officials might close it. Evidence of investments independent of illegal enterprises is therefore needed to support the hypothesis that diversification is one explanation for legitimate business activity.* To achieve the benefits of diversification as defined here—security, and reduction in potential variability of income owing to the risks of illegal enterprise—the businesses should be legally acquired and legally operated.

Although any legitimate investment or wage income can serve the purpose of diversification against the risk of illegal market enterprises, only those jobs, investments, or business holdings openly held and independent of illegal enterprise are considered consistent with efforts to diversify. Only when these conditions are met is the purpose of

---

*The desire for respectability, or status in the community at large rather than the criminal community only, is a reason for entry into legitimate business that might be satisfied by the same investments as those meeting diversification needs, as well as by legitimate businesses used as fronts and tax covers.

diversification fulfilled: to establish a source of income that will continue
for the member or his dependents even in case of death, incarceration,
disfavor with the group, or disruption of illegal market enterprises. A
total of 51 businesses owned by nineteen members of the group with
illegal market income and three jobs held by such members fulfill these
conditions.

More significant than the number of legitimate business holdings that
fulfill the conditions for diversification are the relationships among age,
income-wealth class, and evidence consistent with efforts to diversify.
The data relating income-wealth classes and existence of legitimate
income independent of illegal enterprises are summarized in Table 17.

Of eleven members of the group with illegal market income who have
low or low-to-moderate incomes, three are not known to have any legal
source of income. Another six hold jobs or own small businesses that are
not independent of their illegal market activities and cannot be considered evidence of an effort to diversify. Two do have independent
sources of income, one a job and the other a small business.

Of the eight members of the group estimated to have moderate incomes, two hold jobs and two own business enterprises not associated
with their illegal enterprises. Eight of thirteen moderate-to-high income-
wealth members and eight of eleven high income-wealth members have
investments independent of illegal market enterprises. Among the
wealthier members of the group without independent income it is
possible that some have holdings, such as cash hoards or foreign bank
accounts, protecting them against the risks of illegal enterprises. They
do not, however, have openly held legitimate investments or business
holdings that, for example, would provide a source of income to their

TABLE 17

INCOME-WEALTH CLASS AND INDEPENDENT LEGITIMATE INCOME OF
43 MEMBERS OF THE GROUP WHO HAVE ILLEGAL MARKET INCOME

Income-wealth class	Number without independent income	Number with independent income	Total
Low	3	1	4
Low to moderate	6	1	7
Moderate	4	4	8
Moderate to high	5	8	13
High	3	8	11
Total	21	22	43

dependents on their death, incarceration, or disfavor with the group. Because members of the group have been under investigation by law enforcement officials for some years, their openly held legitimate investments are not likely to have escaped notice; cash hoards and foreign bank accounts are, of course, more difficult to detect.

Although diversification increases with income, some high-income members apparently fail to diversify. Thus while the data support the hypothesis that diversification is one reason for legitimate business investment, they do not show that all members of the group diversify.

Diversification is also an increasing function of age (see Table 18). For those in the moderate-to-high and high income classifications, the percentage without independent income—the percentage failing to diversify—tends to decline with age. If members are grouped in two age categories—under 55 and 55 and over—instead of the five in the table, the percentage failing to diversify drops from 67 for those under 55 years of age to 22 for those 55 and older.

TABLE 18

AGE GROUP AND INDEPENDENT LEGITIMATE INCOME FOR
24 WEALTHIER MEMBERS OF THE GROUP

Age group: moderate-to-high and high income-wealth members	Number without one or more sources of independent income	Number with one or more sources of independent income	Total number	Percentage without one or more sources of independent income
35–44	2		2	100
45–54	2	2	4	50
55–64	2	9	11	18
65–74	1	4	5	20
75 and over	1	1	2	50
Total	8	16	24	

PROFITS

Profit earned without application of the skills and resources peculiar to organized criminal groups is a possible reason for entry into legitimate business. But in such a case, legitimate business investment must compete with marginal rates of return on investment in illegal market enterprises. The economic data on rates of return for both legal and illegal investments is too meager to permit an analysis of this possibility, except to note that the size of the market will eventually limit expansion for any given rate of return. It is possible, however, to determine to what extent the peculiar skills and resources of the group and its individual members that might offer a competitive advantage in legitimate business are actually used, or could be used, in the legitimate businesses they enter.

VII

CRIMINALITY AND LEGITIMATE BUSINESS

Profitability independent of the need to diversify out of illegal market activities is another possible objective of legitimate business activity by members of organized criminal groups. Profitability is of course a primary objective of most legitimate business investments and is not an objective peculiar to members of organized criminal groups. But for members of such groups, legitimate business investment for profit must compete with marginal rates of return on investment in illegal enterprises.

Although rates of return on investment in illegal market enterprises may often be higher than in most legitimate enterprises, marginal rates may be insufficiently high to justify expansion. If this is the case, as it must eventually be where the growth of illegal markets is dependent on the same general factors as growth in legal markets (population, income), and perhaps further limited by law enforcement efforts, it is likely that legitimate investments are an outlet for profits earned in illegal enterprises.

The interesting question is whether certain types of investments, or particular industries, are especially attractive to members of organized criminal groups. Legitimate business investment for profit can be entirely legitimate in both entry and operation, in which case the investments chosen should be independent of any circumstances arising out of criminal activity. But the legitimate investments or lines of trade selected by members of organized criminal groups may be influenced by the circumstances in which illegal market activity, illegal income, and group membership place them.

The circumstances that distinguish members of organized criminal groups from the general population are a peculiar set of skills and resources: a capability for violence and a reputation for the effective use of violence; experience in the corruption of public officials and an established group of corruptees; a cash-rich position, especially illegally earned cash; skills in the evaluation of credit risks, especially borrowers whose loans will not have legal standing; and (possibly) a greater willingness than the general population to engage in criminal activity.

When profit is an objective, members of organized criminal groups may be attracted to businesses in which the peculiar skills and resources of the group and its members (in violence, corruption, the availability of cash, and credit evaluation) offer a competitive advantage. These special skills and resources may also be used to advantage in businesses entered primarily for reasons other than profitability.

VIOLENCE

Violence and a reputation for its effective use are useful in extortion, criminal monopolization of an industry, and labor racketeering.[1] The review of the legitimate business involvements of members of the group in Chapter V identified no instances of extortion or criminal monopolization of an industry. Some members of the group who know labor union leaders have supplied enforcers to them, and in return the group has received assistance from them in finding jobs for members. But no labor union is controlled by members of the group; in fact, two attempts to take over unions have failed.

Only one case of violence apparently related to the conduct of a legitimate business was noted. Thus there is no strong evidence that the Benguerra family or its members use violence in legitimate business, or that this skill or resource is a determinant of the types of legitimate businesses they choose to enter.

The limited use of violence by members of the group may be the result of the policy of its leaders. According to the data sources, this policy is one of opposition to or at least limitations on violence. No details were available on criteria for permitting violence or on success of the leaders in controlling it. Of the violence that occurred in the 1960s (eight known instances) some and possibly all was sanctioned by the group leaders. It is possible that the limited use of violence has led to a decline in the group's reputation for its effective use, if not with loanshark customers at least with labor unions.

CORRUPTION

A network of corruptees and skill in corrupting should be advantageous in obtaining contracts, evading regulations or having regulations such as zoning laws changed, and obtaining licenses or permits. Thus members of organized criminal groups may go into businesses that sell to local government or are regulated by local or even state government.

The use of corruption may be an adjunct to the use of violence in labor racketeering in those instances where the industry involved contracts with the local government, and also in extortion, where the extorted line of trade is subject to licensing or other regulatory control by an agency that can be corrupted.

There are examples in the data sources of benefits to legitimate business ventures of members of the Benguerra family, such as the receipt of government contracts and the changing of zoning regulations, as the result of decisions made by public officials; but it is possible that such decisions were not the result of corruption. One attempt to bribe a regulatory agency was noted.

The bias is such that more instances of corruption in connection with legitimate business, and more systematic corruption, may exist than are reported in the available data sources. But the data do not justify the conclusion that the possibility of using existing corruptees or skills in corruption is an important determinant of the types of legitimate businesses entered by members of the group; rather, one might conclude that corruption and bribery are used when the opportunity presents itself.

ILLEGAL FUNDS

If, as is likely, gambling and loansharking in combination generate a cash flow that cannot be profitably reinvested in those industries, organized criminal groups or the members who operate such enterprises will have large supplies of funds.

These supplies of funds have two characteristics: they are, first, illegal flows that cannot be used openly without being reported for tax purposes and thus partially depleted. Second, this flow may be independent, to some extent, from the supply of funds in legitimate markets. The term "to some extent" is used because conditions in legitimate markets related to high interest rates—lower stock prices, business failures—may reduce the volume of illegal betting and the ability to pay loanshark debts.

A continuous cash-rich position suggests that members of organized criminal groups may have a competitive advantage in industries where providing capital is a means of competing. Especially attractive may be those industries where such capital is not accounted for, the vending machine business, for instance. As discussed earlier, to obtain new locations for machines, vending companies sometimes make interest-free loans to location owners, collecting the loan from proceeds of the vending machine instead of turning over the location owner's portion of the proceeds to him.

A cash-rich position at times when legitimate interest rates are high, or when funds are unavailable at market rates for all who would like to borrow and could normally obtain credit, may lead to relatively large investment by organized criminal groups. Capital would be provided where it would earn the highest return, specifically in those areas where interest rates are differentially high, such as they were in real estate and mortgage lending in the mid-1960s. Members of the group might be expected to invest a larger than average percentage of their available funds in such areas, and where shortages are recurrent, the percentage of the industry's assets controlled by members of organized criminal groups would be expected to grow, at least in the absence of disinvestment. The data were insufficient to consider this possibility.

The open investment of illegally earned funds in legitimate enterprises or securities is limited by the need for protection against a tax evasion charge based on the net worth approach. The individual may increase the amount he can openly invest by reporting on his tax returns profits or income greater than actually earned, a procedure that results, even if indirectly, in the payment of taxes on illegally earned income. Another alternative is the hidden investment where ownership is concealed, so that the use of the funds does not enter into the net worth analysis. In this case taxes are not paid on illegal income before the investment is made. Investments where concealment is possible may thus be favored by members of organized criminal groups, and devices for concealing funds flows (the Swiss bank account, for example) are likely to be used by them. Evidence of hidden investments is necessarily indirect: reports of informants, for example, that a member owns part or all of a business in which he is not among the owners of record.

Illegal funds may also be used to supplement open investments. In the open purchase of a legitimate business or other asset, a portion of the purchase price may be paid in cash on which taxes have not been paid; the seller may report only the openly paid amount, saving himself taxes on the hidden portion. The purchaser's reported profits on resale would be higher than otherwise; taxes and the legitimization of income would be postponed to the time of resale and the tax rate shifted from that on ordinary income to that on capital gains.

Thus the hypothesis presented here is that members of organized criminal groups will be attracted toward businesses or industries in which a cash-rich position provides a competitive advantage, and especially toward those in which hidden investments, or open investments supplemented by illegal funds flows, can be made. One consequence of hidden investment is continued evasion of taxes due on illegal income.

Members of the Benguerra family have a number of legitimate holdings in businesses in which funds can be used that have not been reported for tax purposes. These include businesses in which the investment is entirely hidden, such as casinos; those in which illegal funds can be used as an adjunct to legal funds, as in real estate; and those in which illegal funds can be used to advantage in gaining customers, as in the placement of vending machines. There are also a considerable number of financial institutions that may be important to members of the group for transacting business with illegal funds.

Conspicuous by its virtual absence is investment in areas where the use of illegal funds would not be possible, for example, in publicly traded stocks and bonds. Members have hidden or partially hidden investments in 45 of the 130 businesses held or possibly held in the 1968–1969 period. A total of 56 businesses were judged as involving illegal funds in some way—as hidden investment, as an aid to transactions involving illegal funds, or as an aid to the use of such funds in making loans for legitimate or illegitimate purposes. Thus the data are consistent with the hypothesis that members of the group enter legitimate businesses in which illegal funds can be used to advantage, and that the existence of illegal funds is an important determinant of the types of legitimate business that members of the group enter.

EVALUATION OF CREDIT RISKS

Evaluating borrowers as credit risks for loans lacking legal standing is an area in which members of an organized criminal group involved in loansharking have considerable skills and resources. Borrowing to pay gambling debts is a major category of such loans, and the group has a loose, informal network for checking on the creditworthiness of potential borrowers and discouraging borrowing from more than one firm by a particular borrower.

To take advantage of its skills and position in this area, the organized criminal group may find it attractive to involve itself in legal gambling, as individuals gambling at legal establishments may be unable to borrow from those establishments.

Whether legitimate casinos use the services of members of organized criminal groups in evaluating credit risks is not known, but markers from legitimate casinos are sometimes collected by group members.[2] Legitimate casinos work with travel agencies at times to arrange gambling junkets—vacation packages for gamblers including plane fare, hotel accommodations, meals, and perhaps some free chips for gambling—that are often entirely legal. But a casino faces the problem of evaluating gamblers from another city or country as credit risks, and this function can be taken over by individuals associated with the travel agency booking the junket. (One writer has stated that, during the recession in the first term of the Nixon administration, "only junkets organized by the Mob kept Las Vegas crowded.")[3] The loans are made at loanshark rates and collected after the junketeers return home. The casino may receive a portion of the amount actually collected, rather than the full value of the markers.

An organized criminal group's competitive advantage in evaluating credit risks suggests that control of travel agencies, especially those specializing in gambling junkets, would be attractive. Members of the Benguerra family are involved not only in casino ventures, where illegal funds are used to purchase hidden interests, but also in travel agencies operating gambling junkets. The interesting question here is whether investment in casinos is desirable because of the operation of the casino itself (with the possibility of skimming—failure to report all revenues received), or whether it is primarily the opportunity to lend to gamblers that is the financial attraction in owning casinos. Legalized casino gambling has frequently attracted members of organized criminal groups.

The data available for this study were insufficient to determine the extent to which investment in casinos is attractive because of the opportunities it opens up for making loans to gamblers that are to be collected through a loanshark organization rather than legitimately. Although the issue is not resolvable here, it is relevant to public policy with respect to the legalization of casino gambling, as well as other types of gambling in which the extension of credit is involved.

For the Benguerra family, casino investment and association with travel agencies booking junkets to casinos is the one field of legitimate business that can be considered a group rather than an individual endeavor. Although individuals have arranged or attempted to arrange investments in casinos, one such investment involved participation by several members at the invitation of one of the group's leaders; and the related junkets involved still other members. This is an example, then, of group members acting in concert to use their illegally earned funds not reported for tax purposes in a manner that permits them also to apply their peculiar skills in the evaluation of credit risks for illegal loans, thus expanding their illegal market activities.

The ownership of lending institutions by members and associates may also provide an opportunity for the use of skills in evaluation of credit risks. Illegal loans can be made to customers not qualifying for legal loans, and legal loans can be collected illegally. Loans made to location owners to obtain placement of vending machines is still another activity that employs such skills.

WILLINGNESS TO USE ILLEGAL METHODS

Members of organized criminal groups—at least many of them—probably have a lower aversion to committing criminal acts than the general population. To an individual who already has a criminal record or a reputation for criminal associations, a criminal charge may be less damaging than to an individual with a reputation for integrity. Counteracting this effect is the possibility of a more severe sentence for the prior offender, and the greater probability of apprehension as a result of law enforcement efforts.

Thus members of organized criminal groups may engage in predatory activities in relation to the legitimate world: bankruptcy fraud, insurance fraud, pension fund fraud. They may also sell, at wholesale or retail, stolen, bootlegged, counterfeit, or smuggled goods.

As a general category, businesses in which cheating or evasion of regulations are likely to be profitable and easy to conceal may be attractive: evasion of income and excise taxes, for example. Businesses that present opportunities for skimming may thus be attractive to organized criminal groups. Skimming is, of course, a practice that can be undertaken by anyone operating such a business—a medical practice, a restaurant, a gambling casino. If the tax is on profits, the amount saved is the amount of the unreported revenues times the marginal tax rate.

The data on the Benguerra family do not support the hypothesis that the opportunity to use illegal methods of the type available to anyone in the particular line of trade is an important determinant of legitimate business investment. Eight businesses, owned by members, in which illegal methods of acquisition or operation have been used were identified. But the use of illegal methods was not an organized group endeavor. In only two of the businesses, both of them financial institutions, were the illegal methods standard rather than occasional.

Members of the group are not extensively or systematically involved in predatory activities, either independent of or related to legitimate business enterprise. The city where the Benguerra family operates has been the scene of organized hijacking of trucks and organized bankruptcy fraud, but these activities have been carried on by other criminals, not by members of the group. In fact, the hijacking gang was so well organized during the 1960s that the family made an agreement with them not to abandon hijacked trucks in the section of the city where the group operates. Although stolen merchandise is occasionally bought and resold through retail outlets established by members, it is also at times refused. In one case, however, a member of the group participated with outsiders in the operation of a rather extensive business fraud involving stolen securities. In another case, in the early 1960s, a member of the group arsoned an unprofitable business to collect the insurance. With these exceptions, the group is not known to have been involved in practices in legitimate business that destroy or harm the interests of other parties.

AN OVERVIEW

Table 19 presents an overview of the reasons and objectives for entry into legitimate business by members of the Benguerra family and the peculiar skills and resources employed. The members' legitimate busi-

TABLE 19

SUMMARY OF REASONS FOR ENTRY INTO AND CRIMINALITY IN 130 LEGITIMATE
BUSINESSES OF MEMBERS AND ASSOCIATES OF THE GROUP: 1968–1969

| Category | Total number | | Reasons and objectives | | | | | | Skills and resources | | | | Hidden Investment | Owned by members without income from illegal market activity |
		Tax cover	Support (front)	Services	Diversification	Profit	Violence	Corruption (possible)	Illegal funds	Credit evaluation	Illegal methods		
Eating and drinking places	43	34	17		12	26			8		2	8	1
Other retail trade and services	22	15	7		9	15			2			2	5
Food and kindred products — manufacturing and wholesaling													
Under common management	7	7		1	7	7		1	1		1		
Other	3	1			1	3			1		1	1	1
Construction and building services	6	3			3	6		4	3			3	
Miscellaneous, including trucking	6	4		1	4	6	1	1	2		1	2	
Vending machines and related businesses	12	8		1	7	12			12	7		5	
Casinos and related services	12					12			12	12		12	
Finance, insurance and real estate	16	7			7	16			13	4	3	10	2
Miami investments	3	1			1	3			2			2	
Total	130	80	24	3	51	106	1	6	56	23	8	45	9

ness investments are grouped in major categories. The table notes the
number in each category that serve a particular purpose and the number
in which criminal skills or resources may be involved. It also identifies
holdings of members without income from illegal market activity (gambling, loansharking, and fencing) and holdings in which there are
hidden investments.

It is assumed in Table 19 that any business may provide a tax cover if it is openly held and if the owner of record needs a tax cover, that is, if he has income from illegal market enterprises. It is assumed that a completely hidden investment does not provide a tax cover unless there is information to the contrary. This occurred in one case, where the owner of the hidden interest was receiving a monthly check that was actually a distribution of profit (or a return of invested capital) but appeared to be a fee for services rendered. An openly held investment in which illegal funds are used to supplement legal funds in acquiring a property is assumed to provide a tax cover, either currently or on resale of the property. Jobs held by eight members also provide a tax cover.

Businesses considered as providing support for illegal market enterprises include only those known to be places to do business for owners of retail illegal market enterprises. Excluded are establishments involved in gambling only to the extent that a bet can be placed there.

Businesses providing services to members include only the three noted that place members on the payroll so that they may receive, or appear to receive, a legitimate source of income. Businesses that may serve the purpose of diversification are openly held by members or associates with illegal market income and are not establishments where gambling and loansharking take place. Three of the eight jobs held by members of the group with illegal market income are independent of illegal activities, and thus also provide diversification.

Businesses entered for profit include all businesses except those identified as fronts, although some fronts provide a significant portion of the owner's income through their legitimate operations, and a few legitimate businesses are primarily meeting places for members and are neither fronts nor profit-oriented enterprises. The number of businesses considered profit-oriented thus includes those that may have been entered for diversification or for purposes of a tax cover, unless they are also used as fronts.

Regarding the peculiar skills and resources of the group: the use of illegal funds includes not only hidden and partially hidden investments (identified in a separate column), but also businesses in which illegal funds are used to make loans or businesses that may facilitate the flow of illegal funds.

As Table 19 shows, a legitimate business may serve a variety of purposes and involve the use of one or more skills and resources peculiar to the group and its members. The totals for the various

categories offer another perspective on the group's holdings in legitimate businesses. Of the 130 businesses held or possibly held in the
1968–1969 period, 80 are openly held by members with income from
illegal market activities; 51 are openly held by members with income
from illegal market activities but are independent of that activity,
whereas 24 businesses owned by members (all in retail trade and
services) are used as fronts or as places to do business. There are hidden
investments in 45 of the group's legitimate businesses, and 56 involve
illegal funds in one way or another. The use of illegal funds and the
related skill of credit evaluation (usually also involving illegal funds)
dominate the peculiar skills and resources. In contrast to the use of
illegal funds, only fifteen cases occur in which violence, possible corruption, and illegal methods are used, and in several of these illegal funds
are also involved.

Table 20 relates data on age, income-wealth class, illegal market
activity, and sources of legitimate income for each member. It summarizes much of the data presented in detail earlier. Income or wealth
tends to increase with age and with ownership of a retail, and especially a
wholesale, illegal market enterprise in comparison to employment in
such an enterprise. Employees in illegal enterprises earn legitimate
income from employment or ownership of a small business; but owners
of illegal enterprises tend to obtain legitimate income from ownership of
legitimate business enterprises.

Of the 75 members of the group, two are in jail, fifteen are retired,
three who are neither retired nor in jail have no known source of
legitimate income, nineteen hold jobs providing real income or apparent
legitimate income, and 36 are owners of one or more legitimate
businesses. Thus two-thirds of those with legitimate income obtain that
income as profits (or income from a proprietorship) or dividends rather
than as wages and salaries. Although eighteen members and associates
who are neither in jail nor retired are not known to receive illegal market
income, only seven of them have sources of income that are unrelated to
either illegal market activities or the larger legitimate businesses operated by members of the group.

Joint investments in casino gambling (involving at least six members of
the group), investment in or association with travel agencies, and
lending to gamblers participating in junkets operated by these travel
agencies can be considered a Benguerra family enterprise. There is no
other evidence that the group functions as a firm or an entity with

TABLE 20

AGE, INCOME-WEALTH CLASS, AND SOURCES OF INCOME FOR MEMBERS AND ASSOCIATES OF THE GROUP

Key for income – wealth classes:
L = Low
M− = Low to moderate
M = Moderate
M+ = Moderate to high
H = High

Status or source of legitimate income	Employees: Employment	Employees: Ownership-LB[c]	Employees: None known	Retail owners: Employment	Retail owners: Ownership-LB[c]	Retail owners: None known	Wholesaler/financiers: Employment	Wholesaler/financiers: Ownership-LB[c]	Wholesaler/financiers: None known	In jail	Retired	Employed	Ownership-LB[c]	Total
Members, by age group														
35–44	1L 1M− 1M+			1M−	1M+			1H				1M− 1M		8
45–54	2M	2M	2M−		1M− 1M 2M+			2H				1M	1M	14
55–64	1L 1M−	1M− 1M+	1L		1L 4M+ 1H			5H		1L 1M−	1L 1M	2L 2M	2M	25
65–74		1M−			2M+ 1H			1M+ 1H			1L 7M	1L	1H	16
75 and over				1M+	1M+						4M	1M	1L	7
Unknown												1M	1M 1M+	5
Associates	3M	3M	7M									1M		16
Total for members	7	5	3	2	16	0	0	10	0	2	15	10	5	75
Total for associates	3	3	7	0	0	0	0	0	0	0	0	1	2	16
Total	10	8	10	2	16	0	0	10	0	2	15	11	7	91

a Includes one individual in fencing and five in bookmaking; the others are in numbers gambling, loansharking, or both.
b Four of these ten are also active retailers.
c LB: legitimate business.

respect to legitimate business investment. Members of the group do not need permission to enter legitimate business and are not asked or advised to do so. They freely seek out partners in legitimate ventures among members of the group or outsiders, but their partners (if any) in one enterprise are likely to be different from those in another. The exceptions are close relatives (brothers, for example) who may jointly own and operate an illegal enterprise and one or more legitimate businesses. The largest set of related members involved in joint ownership is a group of four.

Finally, legitimate businesses held by members are not transferred to other members on the death of the member-owner, except in the case of close relatives. Members have at times sold legitimate businesses to other members, but the concerns involved in such a sale are personal rather than group-oriented.

COMPARISON OF LEGITIMATE HOLDINGS AMONG GROUPS OF ORGANIZED CRIME FIGURES

Surveys of legitimate business holdings of organized crime figures are available in the literature on organized crime. The greatest weaknesses in these surveys are in the definition of the subject group (that is, which persons' holdings should be included) and in the exploration of the relationship between the illegal and legitimate enterprises of the subject group.

Donald Cressey considers the legitimate business holdings of the men attending the Apalachin meeting, a gathering of top-level members of organized criminal groups from many different cities in the United States. He states: "The business interests of the men attending the 1957 meeting at the estate of Joseph Barbera in Apalachin, New York, are probably representative of the kinds of legitimate businesses which have been acquired by organized criminals everywhere."[4] These "kinds" include coin-machine businesses; the garment industry; grocery stores; bars and restaurants; olive oil and cheese importing; construction; automobile agencies; coal companies; entertainment; funeral homes; ownership of horses and racetracks; linen and laundry enterprises; trucking; waterfront activities; and bakeries.

A more systematic effort, undertaken for the New York State Identification and Intelligence System (NYSIIS) by Melvin Bers, a labor economist, involved a study of the legitimate business associations and activities of the NYSIIS "target population" of 200 individuals identified as principals and associates of major crime families in the state.[5] Bers' data, despite their problems, are the most systematic available for comparison with the data used for this book—though they are not entirely comparable.

Bers used the files of thirteen regulatory and law enforcement agencies in New York State that cooperate with NYSIIS to gather information on participation of the 200 individuals in legitimate business. "Participation" includes not only openly admitted ownership, but also ownership or control alleged to exist by informants and an unspecified number of instances in which a firm employs an individual who is a member of the target population. Most of the business participation was identified as taking place between 1965 and 1969.

Unfortunately, the 200 individuals in the target population are not identified beyond the fact that they operate in New York State and are apparently of concern to NYSIIS. The group could include all members of the Italian organized criminal groups operating in the state above the lowest rank as defined by these groups, or it could include, as is likely, those considered important by NYSIIS.

The target population also includes "associates" of principals, which is a still more imprecise term: it could include lawyers and accountants or owners of legitimate businesses with whom the principals deal; it could also include major operators of illegal enterprises such as gambling and loansharking who may belong to other ethnic groups. The absence of criteria for inclusion and exclusion in the target group, or, at a minimum, a presentation of the number of people in each of the various possible categories, is the result of unwillingness on the part of NYSIIS to make public the composition of its target population.

A second problem with the study is that it includes no information on the geographical location of the businesses except that most are located in New York State. It is therefore impossible to identify potential monopolization of an industry in a particular geographical area. Bers does, however, provide data on the number of legitimate business participations of each member of the target group. Of the 200 individuals, only eighteen were involved in five or more legitimate businesses; 143 were involved in one to four; and 39 have no such known participation. Bers notes that among those individuals with multiple holdings in legitimate business, the holdings tended to be diversified rather than concentrated in one particular industry. In cases where holdings were concentrated—as in trucking and carting firms involved mainly in waste disposal, trucking in the garment industry, construction, and restaurants and bars—the holdings were associated with connections with labor unions in the respective fields.

Bers does not relate participation in legitimate business to the illegal activities of members of the target group, but he notes that 154 of the 200 were engaged in gambling and 68 (including an unspecified amount of overlap) in loansharking. All were engaged in some form of illegal activity, presumably a criterion for their inclusion in the group.

Bers classifies legitimate business holdings in five groups: (1) legal holdings, legally operated; (2) predatory or parasitic exploitation through the use of coercion, extortion, or fraud; (3) monopoly gain achieved by limiting entry or illegal price fixing; (4) unfair advantage, achieved through control of labor organizations, corruption of public officials, departure from conventional standards prescribed by law, and guarantee of market share by means of intimidation (distinguished from monopoly gains, in that the attempt is a redistribution of profits through price control); and (5) businesses supporting illicit enterprise and receiving reciprocal support, including businesses supporting illegal market enterprises, businesses establishing a legitimate source of income for the individual, and businesses facilitating predatory criminal activity such as outlets for stolen goods. The data collected for the study were insufficient to assign individual businesses to these categories.

Although financial data were limited or nonexistent, Bers concludes from the available information that the identified legitimate business holdings of the target group were small and simple in operation. He suggests that the attempt by those involved in illegal market activities to achieve extra profits through unfair advantage and predatory methods is limited by the risk such techniques entail (risk of loss of legitimate sales and of continued operation in illegal markets) and the fact that such techniques require close control of a firm and are therefore difficult to apply in large firms employing many people.

Table 21 presents a comparison of the two sets of data, those used by Bers and by me, and comparable data for the United States economy by industry division, the broadest SIC code breakdown. Firms in agriculture and mining (as well as the government sector) are excluded from the data for the American economy; neither the NYSIIS target population nor members of the Benguerra family are involved in these industries.

TABLE 21

COMPARISON OF LEGITIMATE BUSINESS ACTIVITY OF THE NYSIIS TARGET GROUP, THE BENGUERRA FAMILY, AND THE UNITED STATES ECONOMY

Industry group	U.S. economy: 1969		NYSIIS target group of 200 (389 firms)		Benguerra family (130 firms)	
	Number (1,000)[a]	Percentage[b]	Number[c]	Percentage[b]	Number[d]	Percentage[b]
Services	2,868	33.9	81	20.8	26	20.0
Retail trade	2,191	25.9	115	29.6	59	45.4
Finance, insurance, and real estate	1,258	14.9	15	3.9	16	12.3
Construction	903	10.7	31	8.0	4	3.1
Wholesale trade	473	5.6	42	10.8	12	9.2
Manufacturing	405	4.8	60	15.4	7	5.4
Transportation, communication, electric, gas, and sanitary services	367	4.3	45	11.6	6	4.6
Total	8,465		389		130	

SOURCES: For the U.S. economy, U.S. Bureau of the Census, *Statistical Abstract of the United States: 1972*, 93rd ed. (Washington, D.C., 1972), table 745, "Proprietorships, Partnerships, and Corporations—Number, Receipts, and Net Profit, by Industry: 1969." For the group of 200, Melvin K. Bers, "The Penetration of Legitimate Business by Organized Crime—An Analysis," Law Enforcement Assistance Administration, U.S. Department of Justice, mimeographed (Washington, D.C., April, 1970), p. 35, table 1, "Participation in Business Firms by 200 Individuals in the NYSIIS Pilot Study Group." For the Benguerra family see above, Chapter V, Table 2, "Legitimate Business Holdings of Members of the Group and Their Associates: Comprehensive List."

[a]Excludes firms in agriculture and mining and those not allocable to individual industry groups. Their inclusion would bring the total to 12,021,000.

[b]Totals may not add to 100 percent due to rounding.

[c]Excludes eighteen firms for which the industry group could not be identified.

[d]Includes firms held or possibly held in the 1968–1969 period; excludes those formerly held.

The holdings of both organized crime populations are more con-centrated in wholesale and retail trade, and less in construction and services, than the American economy as a whole. The NYSIIS group has a greater percentage of firms in manufacturing and transportation than either the Benguerra family or the aggregate economy, but the Benguerra family comes closer to the U.S. average in finance. The two crime samples thus differ from each other as well as from the economy as a whole. The industry divisions are, of course, very broad: services, for example, includes not only personal services such as laundries and barber shops, but also museums and nonprofit membership organizations. Nor does this broad classification provide insight into relationships within the holdings of organized criminal groups, such as that between travel agencies booking junkets for gamblers (a four-digit industry, Arrangement of Transportation, in the Transportation Division) and casinos (a four-digit industry, Amusement and Recreation Not Elsewhere Classified, in the Services Division).

A possible reason for the considerably greater percentage of retail trade in the Benguerra family holdings in comparison to Bers' target population may be the difference in criteria for the inclusion of subjects in the two studies. Bers' target population comprises 200 individuals selected by NYSIIS presumably because their illegal activities are a matter of concern, whereas my study includes all members of an organized criminal group, whether or not they are extensively and successfully involved in criminal activity. Insofar as acquisition of a retail trade establishment may be the first type of legitimate business entered by someone in illegal markets (to provide a front and a tax cover), the inclusion of younger and less successful members in the population of my study can be expected to increase the relative number of retail trade establishments. The successful individual can then seek other outlets for funds earned in illegal enterprises.

In Ianni's study of the "Lupollo" family, he states:

> Current popular opinion has it that the movement of Italian-American criminal syndicates into legitimate business is a recent development. The history of the Lupollo family, however, contradicts this view. Rather than being a recent step, the Lupollo family involvement with legitimate busi-ness began when the family began, almost seventy years ago, and its movement toward legitimation—toward the acquisition or creation of

legal enterprises—seems to have been a steady trend for forty years, and the main motive in the growth of the family empire.[6]

I did not attempt to gather systematically information on the Benguerra family's legitimate business holdings before the decade of the 1960s; the available data sources were inadequate. Occasional references to earlier holdings include one case of business ownership by members or former members dating to the 1930s; two cases in the 1940s; and four in the 1950s. The simultaneous entry of members of organized criminal groups into legtimate and illegal businesses is consistent with the hypotheses that legitimate business provides benefits such as a tax cover, support for illegal market enterprises, and diversification against the risks of illegal activities.

Ianni found that the legitimate business empire of the Lupollo family is a cohesive syndicate comprising eleven interconnected enterprises involved in transportation, trucking, waste disposal, real estate, public relations, fuel supply, and food manufacturing and distribution, with combined assets in excess of $30 million. (He notes, however, that he has sometimes misidentified the product or service supplied by a company to protect the anonymity of the family.)[7] In addition, he identified ten family-related enterprises in real estate, plumbing, construction, financial services, clothing manufacture, linen supply, beauty shops, vending machines, and travel agencies—a selection essentially consistent with the pattern of legitimate business investment of the Benguerra family. In addition, members of the Lupollo family own legitimate enterprises independent of the family empire.

Members of the Lupollo family operate a lay-off service for eight independent retail numbers enterprises, for which they also provide police protection. They receive a percentage of the gross (or the total amount bet) from each enterprise. Only one of the retail enterprises is owned by a member of the family; five are owned by people related to the family; and two were sold to Puerto Ricans. Ianni does not use the term "owned," but he notes that receipts of the various enterprises are not co-mingled; and although these enterprises are "fully guaranteed"[8] by the family, they are actually loaned funds only in emergencies. This structure appears similar to that of the Benguerra family's numbers industry, where several independent firms also exist—except that the

Benguerra family provides a nonmandatory lay-off service and controls (or attempts to control) entry.

In loansharking the situation is similar, except that competition from other ethnic minorities is absent. Members of the Lupollo family finance loansharking and may exercise some control at the retail level, but again only one member is active at that level.

Ianni found that funds flows took place through individuals among illegal and legitimate enterprises. Real estate and financial investment firms are the means by which members of the Lupollo family "cleanse" or legitimatize funds and make use of illegal funds flows. These enterprises provide a tax cover and a means for using illegal funds for profit. Although Ianni states that money is reinvested in loansharking after it is cleansed, this is unlikely; loansharking does not require clean money, and is in fact an ideal outlet for income not reported on tax returns if the market is sufficient to allow for reinvestment of illegal earnings.

Ianni's subject group is composed of fifteen men who run the family business empire, legal and illegal; but this group does not include the second and third levels—supervisory and other employees—nor does it include the operators of the numbers and retail loanshark enterprises, or the legitimate business investment of these operators. The only family member active in retail numbers and loansharking has a storefront from which he operates.

Ianni thus does not present data allowing a determination of whether ownership and operation of retail illegal market enterprises is a reason for legitimate business entry. The members of the family do have illegal market income; they do have legitimate businesses that can serve as tax covers; they have entered industries where their illegal funds can be effectively used. They apparently do not make use of their skills and resources in violence or their presumed willingness to use illegal methods in legitimate business; they may or may not use corruption. Ianni provides no evidence indicating that family members are involved in casinos or other legalized gambling.

In summary, the available comparative literature offers a reasonably consistent portrayal of the types of legitimate businesses in which members of organized criminal groups are active. The results of these studies can be compared only roughly or partially with the results of my study. Ianni's work defines carefully the members of the group included in his analysis, but they include only the top-level members of a closely-knit family and exclude the owners and operators of illegal enterprises run by the family. Bers' study and the observations offered by Cressey fail to provide a precise definition of the populations under study and do not relate data on legitimate business investment to illegal market activity. There is no systematic survey other than that of this study of the legitimate business holdings of a defined subject group that also provides sufficient detail to examine the relationship between illegal activities and legitimate business holdings.

VIII

ORGANIZED CRIME AND PUBLIC POLICY

This book uses concepts from the fields of sociology and political science as well as economics to explain some aspects of the Benguerra family's activities and the behavior of its members. It was not my original intent to draw so heavily on disciplines other than economics; it simply became necessary to do so. The problem of organized crime, like many other problems, requires a multidisciplinary approach, both theoretically and in the application of findings to public policy.

Thus the concept of a quasi-government is used to describe certain functions performed by the group that go beyond those of a cartel. The need for definition and protection of property rights as part of an economic system is recognized in economic theory and is generally considered a function of government.[1] The economic benefits of establishing a successful quasi-government are apparent in its ability to reduce the risks of organized criminal activity and internalize the costs of otherwise uncontrolled behavior (especially violence). But explanations for the means by which Italian organized criminal groups have succeeded in establishing and maintaining quasi-governments was sought from the field of sociology, in the cultural background of Italian-Americans from southern Italy.

In understanding the ethnic succession that has taken place in organized crime and is continuing through the takeover of some illegal markets by members of non-Italian minorities, concepts from sociology and political science may have greater value than economic explanations. An economic theory of ethnic succession would be based on changes in opportunities available to ethnic minorities, and that is no doubt part of the explanation. The economic approach explains difficulties in recruiting capable new members, but it does not explain why organized criminal groups retain an ethnic identity, or why groups of different ethnic backgrounds continue to coexist in the same cities.*

The ethnic identity of members of an organized criminal group appears critical for forming the sociological basis on which a quasi-government can be created, legitimatized, and made acceptable to the members. Ethnic succession in organized crime is thus a consequence not only of changing economic opportunities, but also of the differing abilities of various groups to establish and maintain the quasi-governments that make them effective competitors in illegal markets. The success of different groups in controlling violence, their solidarity in the face of law enforcement, and their success in corrupting the criminal justice system depend on the cultural factors peculiar to the particular ethnic minority. These cultural factors influence the behavior not only of those who choose criminal careers, but also of those members of that particular ethnic minority who are in positions of power in government and in the criminal justice system.

The purpose here is to explore the public policy implications of the findings of this study: whether efforts to combat organized criminal activity should be expanded, reduced, or reallocated, and what specific strategies of law enforcement might be adopted. It is worthwhile first to take a brief look at recent developments in law enforcement itself.

Efforts to combat organized crime have increased considerably since the early 1960s. The federal government has increased both its level of effort and its jurisdiction, and new organizational modes—strike forces—have been developed to improve cooperation among federal agencies and among federal, state, and local agencies.

In 1961 Congress passed (and has since amended) the Travel Acts,[2] which expanded the jurisdiction of the federal government and defined as criminal certain activity related to the sale of illegal goods and services other than that sale itself, such as transmitting information related to betting across state lines, and crossing state lines to promote crimes of

---

*Another process at work is the tendency of older, successful members of organized criminal groups to become more averse to the risks of criminal activity. In the absence of competition from other groups and recruitment difficulties, this process should result in conflict within groups between younger and older members and, possibly, the establishment of new groups of the same ethnic minority with younger membership. This process may be behind the internal problems that have arisen in the Italian underworld in New York City in the last several years.

gambling, narcotics, bootlegging, bribery, and extortion. Title III of the Omnibus Crime Control and Safe Streets Act of 1968[3] provided for court-ordered wiretapping and electronic surveillance.

The Organized Crime Control Act of 1970[4] included provisions for witness immunity and protection; extended federal jurisdiction over illegal gambling businesses and gambling-related corruption; provided for increased sentences for dangerous special offenders; and made it unlawful to invest income or the proceeds of income derived from a pattern of racketeering activity in enterprises engaged in interstate commerce. (Racketeering is broadly defined as felonious violation of various state and federal laws relating to gambling, loansharking, and narcotics, as well as activities such as kidnapping, arson, bribery, and extortion.) Criminal penalties include not only fines and prison terms, but seizure of property.* A possible consequence of the legislation is greater hidden and less open investment.

One of the government's tools for combatting organized crime—the federal wagering tax statutes—were partially invalidated by a series of Supreme Court decisions in 1968 (*Marchetti* v. *United States* and *Grosso* v. *United States*) and 1971 (*United States* v. *United States Coin and Currency*),[5] which held that the self-incrimination clause of the fifth amendment to the Constitution could be used as a defense against failure to comply with the registration requirements of the federal wagering tax law and in wagering tax forfeiture cases.[6] A possible outcome of the precedent established by these cases is a lessened need for tax covers for illegal income, and instead a shift to simply reporting income as miscellaneous.

The federal government has also greatly expanded its resources devoted to combatting organized crime. The Department of Justice began a concerted drive against organized crime in the early 1950s, and in 1954 its Organized Crime and Racketeering Section (OCRS) was established.[7] In 1957 the section had ten attorneys; by 1969 it had 85. Table 22 presents typical government statistics on law enforcement against organized crime. These statistics are measures of input or level

---

*The Advisory Task Force on Organized Crime, one of the several task forces reporting to the National Advisory Commission on Criminal Justice Standards and Goals, discussed the question of further legislation on organized crime at its various meetings during 1972. The task force members, of whom I was one, were in general agreement that with the passage of the Organized Crime Control Act of 1970, the legislation needed by the federal government to pursue an aggressive policy of combatting organized crime was on the books, and that most if not all state legislatures had passed or were considering legislation needed at that level.

of effort (number of attorneys employed, days in court) and measures of output (indictments and convictions). As the table shows, the level of effort increased considerably between 1960 and 1969, and indictments and convictions also generally increased.

Organizationally, the government's effort against organized crime is carried out through strike forces. The strike force is a cooperative effort among investigators and attorneys from the various federal agencies that have jurisdiction over matters related to organized crime, including the FBI and the Intelligence Division of the Internal Revenue Service. Each strike force is headed by an attorney from OCRS and operates in a particular city. The first strike force was established in Buffalo in 1966. The number of strike forces increased from five to thirteen during fiscal 1970.[8] By 1971 there were nineteen in major cities throughout the United States, but only fifteen in early 1978. The number of attorneys in OCRS is thus only a partial measure of the increased effort devoted to fighting organized crime; over half the manpower of the strike forces in 1970 was provided by the Internal Revenue Service.[9]

The strategy of the strike forces has been primarily that of attrition. In 1963 an attorney with OCRS described the section's strategy as simply "to identify, prosecute, and convict persons actively engaged in organized crime."[10] By 1970 the avowed strategy was to concentrate on illegal gambling as a major source of funds for organized crime and on corruption of public officials.[11] But in 1977 the General Accounting Office reported that organized crime was flourishing in spite of the $80 million a year budget for fighting it and the conviction of 9,411 organized crime figures since 1962; by that time OCRS had 110 attorneys and intended to add another 35. In 1978 organized crime fighters in the Carter administration claimed a switch in basic strategy away from a case-by-case, headhunting approach. Instead, they planned to put greater emphasis on attacking criminal control of legitimate businesses and labor unions and to develop cases that would eliminate entire enterprises controlled by organized crime.

When asked about the size of organized crime, the Assistant Attorney General in charge of the Criminal Division of the Department of Justice, Benjamin Civiletti, could only say, "I wish I knew. Frankly, I don't think the things I have seen provide any reasonable estimate of the dollar cost of organized crime or the number of its violations."[12] The need is still for statistics not about law enforcement but about organized criminal activity itself, by which the government's new legislation and its expanding level of effort can be evaluated.

TABLE 22

Organized Crime and Racketeering Section (OCRS), U.S. Department of Justice: Staff, Work Days, Convictions, Indictments, 1960–1969

	Fiscal year									
	1960	1961	1962	1963	1964	1965	1966	1967	1968	1969
Number of OCRS attorneys	17	37	52	60	63	54	48	54	65	85
Days in field	660	2434	5057	6177	6699	4432	3480	4494	6886	9570
Days before grand jury	100	518	894	1353	677	605	373	419	402	746
Days in court	61	116	329	1081	1364	813	606	612	1123	1490
Number of defendants indicted	n.a.[a]	49	154	436	683	706	994	1107	1166	813
Number of defendants convicted	n.a.[a]	49	117	350	619	468	457	400	520	449

Source: "The Strike Force: Organized Law Enforcement v. Organized Crime," *Columbia Journal of Law and Social Problems*, 6:3, p. 504. Statistics for 1969 are influenced by the Supreme Court decisions on the federal wagering tax statutes and the reassignment of narcotics violations from OCRS to another section.
[a]Statistics not available.

One conclusion of this study is that the Benguerra family is neither of major significance in the economy of the city where it operates nor a serious threat to its legitimate business competitors or the customers of its legal and illegal enterprises. Loansharking involves the implicit threat of violence in collecting debts and the possible inducement of debtors to use a variety of means, some illegal, to obtain funds to pay debts; but the actual use of violence is infrequent. The numbers industry involves neither violence nor fraud—gamblers know what the payoff rates are, the winning number is not fixed, and bettors are paid the amount they expect to receive when they win. But the prices charged by the firms in the industry are monopoly prices, and the group's illegal gambling enterprises are associated with extensive corruption of the local police and other public officials both within and outside the criminal justice system.

None of the major reasons for entry of members of the group into legitimate business—to acquire tax covers, establish fronts, and diversify—in itself leads to damage to competitors, consumers, or taxpayers. The group's legitimate business activities are not generally predatory and cannot be characterized as an aggressive effort to achieve profits through illegal means. The use of violence in legitimate business is minimal, and corruption only occasional. The group's illegal markets are local ones and their network of corruptees is also local, tied to a specific geographical area. This perhaps discourages consumer fraud of the fly-by-night type such as that occurring in the home-improvement industry, in which the perpetrators flee from one jurisdiction to another to avoid apprehension.

Although many members of the group earn substantial incomes, not all are financially successful. Members are not involved in illegal drug markets and only infrequently in predatory activities such as the sale of stolen merchandise. They are not aggressive in expanding illegal markets, nor is there evidence for creativity in seeking out new ones.

Nevertheless, the city where the Benguerra family operates is one of the eighteen in which a full-fledged federal strike force was established in the late 1960s, presumably with the goal of controlling organized crime thereby prosecuting members of the group as well as other individuals. The presumed dangers and consequences of organized criminal activity are what has led to the considerable increase in federal resources devoted to fighting it and to the passage of new legislation. In 1974 Supreme Court Justice William Rehnquist used "the heavy utilization of our domestic banking system by the minions of organized crime as well as by millions of legitimate businessmen" as partial justification for the Supreme Court's decision to uphold the constitutionality of the Bank Secrecy Act of 1970, legislation that unquestionably has its costs in privacy by giving the government extensive access to bank customer records.[13]

Three questions arise with respect to public policy and organized crime: whether the resources and legislation directed toward organized crime control ought to be increased and extended, or decreased; how these resources ought to be allocated; and what specific goals and strategies might be used to deal with organized crime in a particular city or a particular illegal market.

If the activities of the Benguerra family are representative of the activities of other organized criminal groups in the United States, it is questionable whether the current level of resources devoted to fighting organized crime is warranted, and it is especially doubtful that fears of organized crime should be used to justify legislation involving incursions into privacy and the potential for abuse, as does the Bank Secrecy Act.

It is, of course, possible that organized crime in other cities—whether controlled by Italians or by other ethnic minorities—is far more serious than it appears to be in the city studied here. Many groups in the country are considered by law enforcement officials more violent and more likely to be involved in predatory activities than the Benguerra family. Members of organized criminal groups have been involved in a wide range of predatory activities, and volumes have been filled with organized crime horror stories. These anecdotes are often presented as examples, with the implication that they are the tip of an iceberg.[14] If there are cities in the United States where it can be shown that violence and predatory methods are characteristic of the operation of organized criminal groups, law enforcement resources should perhaps be directed toward eliminating these serious consequences.

Systematic studies of a number of organized criminal groups in different cities would thus be useful in determining whether the current emphasis on the problem of organized crime is appropriate, and how resources to combat it ought to be allocated among different cities. Data on organized crime in other cities comparable to those used for this study—no doubt with the same weaknesses for this purpose—exist in the files of organized crime intelligence units at federal, state, interstate, and local levels. It would obviously be desirable to be able to make better estimates of the size of illegal market enterprises and the investment in legitimate enterprise. Although information in intelligence units is gathered for the purposes of prosecution and conviction, it is nevertheless the most systematic information likely to be available. Its adequacy could be improved considerably by gathering types of information usually overlooked by investigators.

Finally, the level of activity and the extent of predatory behavior of members of any organized criminal group is at least in part a consequence of prior law enforcement efforts. In the city in question, the level of the federal effort increased somewhat during the 1960s; another expansion took place near the end of the period 1968–1969 with the establishment of a federal strike force. The effects of the strike force therefore postdate the period analyzed in this book but would be significant in analyzing the activity and behavior of the group during the 1970s. During the 1960s, local law enforcement agencies affected the group more than did federal, especially since much of the legislation expanding federal jurisdiction over organized criminal violations had not yet been passed. It is possible that during the 1960s the local authorities were successful in employing a law enforcement strategy that permitted the group to operate in illegal markets in return for restricting violence and predatory activity.

Law enforcement strategy against organized crime has been directed toward identifying members of organized criminal groups—especially Italian ones—and attempting to prosecute and convict members and especially leaders. The headhunting strategy has been encouraged by the journalistic attention given to leaders of organized crime and by the fact that evaluation of an agency's efforts to combat crime is based primarily on its success in bringing indictments and obtaining convictions, rather than on changes it may have brought about in the extent or seriousness of the problem.

The following discussion of strategies for dealing with an organized criminal group that operates as does the Benguerra family is speculative and is not intended as a comprehensive program for combatting organized crime. It is intended, rather, to highlight three basic points. First, the success of law enforcement agencies in fighting organized crime (and thus the justification for the resources they use and the legislation under which they operate) should be based on their effect on the harm and dangers of organized criminal activity, not on the number of indictments and convictions they bring. Second, alternative strategies for dealing with organized crime, or an organized criminal group or illegal market, involve tradeoffs: reducing some of the undesirable consequences of organized crime often worsens other consequences, and alternative strategies should be realistic in considering the conditions that could be brought about by the various alternatives. Finally, the establishment of goals for an organized crime control program and a strategy to achieve them requires value judgments about the seriousness of the various consequences of organized criminal activity.

The two most undesirable consequences of the activities of the Benguerra family, are, in my view, its corruption of local police and other public officials both within and outside the criminal justice system, and the high prices it charges for numbers gambling. Prices are as high or higher in other cities; and paying off the police and other criminal justice officials goes hand-in-hand with illegal gambling operations. Because a large portion of the general public, the police, and public officials do not consider gambling an activity that is in itself evil or immoral, and because many people want to gamble, it is probably impossible to eradicate gambling altogether and with it the related corruption of the criminal justice system. Prosecution of individuals active in illegal gambling often fails to stop these activities for more than a day or so. Even if all members of a group active in illegal gambling were incarcerated, the market would probably be taken over by other groups. A periodic effort to enforce laws against illegal gambling should increase the costs of doing business, but it is also likely to increase prices and police corruption.

The group is typical in monopoly pricing in its illegal numbers enterprises and in corrupting local police and public officials. It is possibly unusual in its limited use of violence and predatory criminal activity, limited use of illegal methods in legitimate business, lack of aggression in expanding illegal markets and developing new ones, and peaceful cooperation with other criminal groups in the same city.

On the one hand, an aggressive policy of law enforcement against leaders of the group could bring to power younger leaders, more aggressive and willing to use violence. If, on the other hand, enough high-ranking members of the group could be successfully prosecuted to demonstrate the leaders' inability to protect members from law enforcement and destroy the group's ability to control its members and its illegal markets, the effort might be worthwhile. Law enforcement would then have to deal with new entrants competing to take over the disrupted group's illegal markets, a situation that could be accompanied by violence, consumer fraud, and continued corruption of the local police force.

Whether a law enforcement strategy could be devised that would reduce or eliminate gambling-related police corruption and at the same time increase payouts to bettors without encouraging fraud or violent competition is a speculative question. A policy of nonenforcement of the law would eventually reduce police corruption and corruption at other levels in the criminal justice system: bribes would not be paid indefinitely for services not needed. But new entrants would be encouraged, and existing organized criminal groups would probably turn to violence to control entry in the absence of the collusion with the police on which they can currently depend. New entrants might also establish numbers enterprises using methods of generating the winning number that could be fixed, thus leading to fraudulent operations.

A more refined strategy would be to enforce the law only against those numbers enterprises that were either fraudulent or failed to raise payouts to bettors to a specified percentage—perhaps 80 percent. The

greatest problem here would be subversion by the local police unwilling
to give up income they receive in the form of bribes. If the strategy were
successful in raising payouts throughout the city, law enforcement
officials might have to assist existing operators in preventing competition from newcomers or accept the use of violence to control entry. The
strategy is in fact a strategy for regulating an illegal industry: setting
prices, enforcing fairness and honesty, and controlling entry. In addition to reducing police corruption and raising payout rates, profits to
operators would also be reduced.

The more obvious way to achieve the same ends is, of course, to
legalize gambling. The technology of illegal numbers gambling is
simple; bets are often taken by numbers writers who contact each bettor
individually, and labor costs are high. (High labor costs may be the one
economic factor limiting the illegal numbers industry by making it
impossible to offer payouts competitive with those for other forms of
gambling.) A legal numbers industry would perhaps eliminate the
roving writer and sell bets only as other low-value, frequently purchased
items are now sold—at newspaper and cigarette stands, through vending
machines, and also probably by telephone. Bettors might also be offered
a wider range of ways to bet, so that on some bets the payoff would be
lower but the probability of winning greater. The technology of a legal
numbers industry is thus likely to be quite different from that of the
illegal numbers industry.

One of the problems with the legalization of gambling is the opportunity for loansharking created by gambling. This arises because gambling debts are not legal debts, and the procedures used to collect debts
legally are not available to the creditor. One solution would be to give
gambling debts legal standing. Although this would not eliminate the role
of the loanshark in lending to individuals not judged creditworthy by
legitimate financial institutions, it would reduce gambling-related loanshark activity considerably. For organized criminal groups whose primary
illegal activities are gambling and loansharking, the legalization of
gambling might eliminate the major illegal activity that provides in-
centive for the group to organize, thus reducing the ability of its
members to function successfully in the loanshark industry even if many
of them became involved in legal gambling enterprises.

Insofar as legitimate business interests are concerned, the minimal use
by the group of predatory methods does not support a strategy of
attempting to drive members out of legitimate business. The greatest

potential for harmful illegal operation of legitimate businesses exists in the holdings of members of the group in financial institutions—an area that might be worth increased attention by investigators. Although members of the group have been unsuccessful in their two attempts to gain control over labor unions, their interest in doing so suggests that continued attention by investigators to this problem would probably also be worthwhile.

Appendix
RESEARCH METHODS AND DATA SOURCES

Research on organized crime is difficult. Participants don't want to talk about their activities or admit involvement, if indeed they can even be identified. The organizations that gather systematic data on organized criminal activities are almost exclusively law enforcement agencies whose purpose is to identify and prosecute violations of the law, rather than to provide data banks for social scientists. Even when they allow access to their files, which is rare, the data are not likely to be those the researcher would have chosen. In spite of some excellent investigative journalism, information about organized criminal activity available to most of us most of the time comes primarily from the daily news media and is highly anecdotal.

It is an obligation, therefore, of any serious writer who presents an analysis of even a selected segment of organized criminal activity in the United States to explain where the information for the study came from, how it was handled, and problems that were encountered.

Once, the decision had been made to do a case study of an organized criminal group, my next step was to select the group. Three criteria were used: first, it was decided that the group should be the dominant organized criminal group in the city where it operated and that its operations should be more or less self-contained, so that the factors influencing its activities, especially its legitimate business involvement, would be identifiable. This criterion eliminated the five groups operating in New York City, because cooperation and conflict among them would have required studying all of them simultaneously.

Second, it was decided that the group should be important enough to warrant study; and third, that it should be one of the groups on which the most comprehensive data were likely to be available. The group selected is Italian because Italian groups have dominated organized crime in the United States for some decades. This dominance is probably exaggerated by the press and law enforcement officials, but it does exist; and the attention given to Italian organized criminal groups also means that the data on them are more comprehensive than data on others. The specific group was selected after consultation with representatives of the federal agency that made the data available; it is one of the groups on which the agency considered its data most comprehensive.

Of the nineteen groups outside New York City identified as of 1967, some have as few as twenty members (President's Commission on Law Enforcement, *Task Force Report: Organized Crime*, p. 7). Published figures on the number of members of different groups are not available, but estimates can be made for some from the information provided by government agencies and published in books such as Reid's *Grim Reapers* and Mollenhoff's *Strike Force*. These books provide charts listing the names and positions of some members of some groups; where the charts stop at the level of "section leader," for example, the size of the group can be estimated by assuming that there are perhaps ten unlisted members in each section. Only some of the New York City groups apparently have several hundred members. With its 75 members, the Benguerra family falls in a medium-sized class of 50–200 members—a class that includes groups in several cities. The city in which the family operates also has organized criminal groups of other ethnic minorities, as do several other cities.

The city in which the Benguerra family operates is not identified, to allow fuller presentation of data than would otherwise be possible. A considerable amount of information was originally obtained by investigators from informants; identification of the city would make possible identification of specific people involved in specific incidents, and thus possibly identify the informants. Concealment of the identity of the city means that some information about the group from published federal, state, and local government documents, newspaper and magazine articles, and interviews with law enforcement officials cannot be explicitly documented because this would identify the city. To avoid identification of the group, some information—specific dates of events and specific amounts of money—have been generalized. Thus it may be mentioned that an event took place in the mid-1960s or that a business was sold for \$40–50,000. In all these cases the information given is accurate; it is less precise than it might have been, but it has not been distorted.

In summary, the group selected is one of the major Italian organized criminal groups outside New York City. It operates in one of the twenty largest cities in the United States. In size and in its coexistence with organized criminal groups of other ethnic minorities in the same city it is not unique, although to call it typical would be too strong.

The primary data sources for this study were provided by a federal agency. The data were gathered during spring and summer 1970 by abstracting information from government reports. The information as presented in these reports is neither organized nor analyzed. A particular report (of which there were hundreds) might include information on a number of matters—an illegal market operation, ownership of a legitimate business, membership in the group—with no cross-referencing to other reports where the same matters are considered. A great deal of sorting out and collating was therefore necessary. Occasional documents summarizing information from the reports were available, but like the reports themselves, the information they offer is descriptive and factual; no estimates or projections are made and no conclusions drawn.

The reports include information based on surveillance, information from informants, reports of occasional conversations of law enforcement officials with members of the group, and information from state and local government agencies and private agencies such as credit bureaus. The information from public and private agencies includes items such as records of real estate transactions, information obtained from credit bureaus, the location of vending machines placed by a firm owned by members of the group, and information on incorporation filed with the state department of corporations.

As examples of surveillance, a report might note that a particular individual was observed by the investigator to be present at and operating a particular legitimate business, such as a grocery store; or that a particular individual was observed driving an automobile with a license number registered to some other individual.

Information from informants is diverse. An informant may report on a variety of matters: induction of members into the group, the desire of a particular person to join, the refusal of a member to buy stolen goods to sell in his store, the "take" in a gambling enterprise, the possible ownership of a legitimate business by a member of the group, the decision to close a casino gambling operation because of the high payoffs wanted by the police to permit the operation to continue. The reports do not identify informants by name, although some general description is sometimes given. There was no indication that any informant was a member of the group.

Informants provided a significant portion of the information available in the data sources. Although statements of informants are factually reported there, the information they provide is not necessarily accurate; in legal terms it is often hearsay. Because informants are not identified, it is not possible to determine whether items of information from separate reports were provided by the same informant. Thus it was not possible, with the information the federal agency made available to me, to analyze the internal consistency of information provided by a particular informant or to compare the totality of information from one informant with that from another.

But information from informants can sometimes be verified through the records of private or public agencies. Less dependable verification occurs through the reporting of the same information by different informants, possibly at different periods in time; it is often possible to establish that information has been provided by more than one source because of the general backgrounds of the informants (sex, domicile, type of employment) or because the information overlaps—the two sources are consistent but each has information the other does not have. Another consideration is overall consistency of the information.

In most cases no item of information from an informant was included in the data base unless it was verified by another source or informant. When reports were sufficiently detailed to suggest that the source had at least secondhand knowledge of an event, however, the information was included. Information reported as rumor was excluded unless verified by other information. For example, if it was reported that a particular member was rumored to be a partial owner of a legitimate business, such an item was not included in the data base. But if it was later reported that the member wished to sell or had sold his interest in the business, the earlier report was considered verified and both items were included.

At times statements of informants were contradictory. This occurred on occasion over the question of membership, where a third item of information was usually available to confirm one of the others. In one instance an individual was reported to be a member and on a later occasion was reported eager to become a member. The description of the individual's activity and behavior in this case was more consistent with close associate status than membership; and expression of eagerness to become a member was considered unlikely to come from a member. The individual was classified as a close associate.

As this example shows, it was necessary to exercise judgment at many points in selecting, rejecting, or classifying information for the data base. The standards of degree of detail, verification by another source, and consistency proved sufficient to determine the majority of decisions. Were the same data available to another researcher, it is likely that the differences in results would be minor.

The primary data sources were supplemented by a three-day field trip in summer 1970 to the city where the group operates. During the field trip I observed about a dozen of the legitimate businesses owned by members, primarily to determine whether they were large, flourishing businesses or smaller establishments. Notes were taken on matters that could be easily observed: the number of delivery trucks outside a food-processing establishment, the seating capacity and prices of a restaurant, customers present, the physical size of a plant, the merchandise available in a retail trade establishment.

Many interviews were conducted, not with members of the group, but with people in the law enforcement community. Several interviews with federal and state law enforcement officials took place in the city during the three-day field trip. Private citizens concerned with the problem of organized crime there and a lawyer who had defended a member of the group were also interviewed. Many more interviews were conducted in Washington, D.C., and New York City between 1969 and 1971. Those interviewed included law enforcement officials with the United States Departments of Justice, the Treasury, and Labor; law enforcement officials in state organized crime intelligence systems; members of the staffs of state and federal legislative committees or commissions established to deal with organized crime; representatives of citizens' crime commissions; members of private consulting firms involved in projects bearing on organized crime; and reporters for various news media who specialize in investigative reporting on organized crime.

Some of the interviews, especially those conducted during the field trip, concerned the Benguerra family. Others concentrated on the activities of other groups, and a considerable number were wide-ranging and covered a variety of organized crime matters, law enforcement problems, and problems of research on organized crime. The people interviewed gave generously of their time and effort in discussing ideas about organized crime, communicating the knowledge they had gained from their own experiences in combatting it, and suggesting possible sources of information.

A few public documents published by federal, state, and local government agencies also include information about the group in this study. Information in such publications often is either anecdotal or a summary of organized crime conditions or problems; seldom is documentation offered. Statements in publications of this type, like general statements about the group made in interviews, are viewed as the opinions and judgments of law enforcement officials and were not used as basic data; where such opinions and judgments are used in the text they are identified as such.

My primary source of data was thus the reports made available by a federal agency. These reports did not include any information from federal or state tax returns, and the legal restrictions on the availability of tax returns made it impossible to obtain such information. Nor was it possible to obtain information on the legitimate businesses owned by members of the group and their associates—even aggregate figures on sales, for example—from the Census of Manufactures taken by the Bureau of the Census. In 1970 Dun and Bradstreet listed only nine of the legitimate businesses held by members of the group; none was given a credit rating. I reviewed court records on two cases involving group members and found them unproductive as a source of data.

The data sources available offered some information for the entire period of 1960–1970. A variety of data had been collected about the group; my emphasis was on identifying members and their close associates, illegal market activities of members, and legitimate business investments of members and close associates. The years 1968–1969 were chosen for comprehensive description because they are the years for which the most complete data are available—partly because of the increased investigative efforts during these years. Thus some legitimate business ownership, for example, is reported for this period, but it is only sometimes possible to determine that the business was owned in an earlier time period.

The data sources available made possible the most comprehensive data base about the illegal market activities and legitimate business investments of the members of an organized criminal group that has ever, as far as I know, been developed for research purposes. Nevertheless, the sources were designed for law enforcement purposes, and not all the information that would be desirable for a study of this kind was available. Often, for example, information indicating the size of a legitimate business—financial data, description of the establishment's size, number of people employed, number of customers—was lacking. (As mentioned above, to get a better idea of size, I visited about a dozen of these businesses.)

Whether or not the data are complete, especially in the three areas of membership, illegal market enterprises, and legitimate business activities, cannot be known with certainty. Members may be involved in various activities that have not come to the attention of either the public or the law enforcement agencies collecting information on the group. However, the group has been observed more or less intensively since at least 1961 by federal investigators. As far as membership is concerned, the data sources offer information not only on individuals identified as members but also on their close associates, although not in as great detail. Some of these associates may actually be members. Certain close associates, selected according to criteria explained earlier, were included in the analysis at times. It is therefore unlikely that there are important members of the group who have not been included in the analysis at least as associates.

The data on legitimate business holdings and investments of members of the group are likely to be incomplete. This is especially true of investment where ownership is concealed and the investment is not reported on tax returns. Assets openly held (reported for tax return purposes) are less likely to escape identification, because the same effort is not made to conceal ownership, and documents confirming ownership may exist. When day-to-day operating control is not exercised, the information may nevertheless be incomplete because tax return data were not available for this study. For example, some retired members of the group make frequent visits to stockbrokers, but there is no information available on their holdings of securities.

The data on legitimate businesses that are directly managed by members of the group probably involve very few, if any, omissions, because day-to-day operating control is observable by investigators.

In the area of legitimate business ownership and legitimate investment, investigators could probably obtain additional information if they considered it worthwhile to do so. This is less likely to be the case with illegal market activity because investigative efforts behind the data sources are directed toward the identification of criminal activity. Over time, involvement in illegal enterprises, which are daily rather than sporadic criminal activity, is likely to come to the attention of investigators. Absence of any known criminal activity by a member is often specifically noted in the reports. The information on illegal enterprises is lacking not in whether a member is engaged in gambling or loansharking, but on the size of these enterprises—the volume of business, the number of people employed, the number of customers, and revenues and expenses. Efforts were made to develop estimates on the basis of the information that was available.

Some of the material used to support or contradict hypotheses about organized crime involves events rather than analysis of the systematic data on membership and legal and illegal activities. Unlike legitimate business ownership and the operating of illegal market enterprises, these events are not continuing and recurring. For example, on one occasion the boss of the group arbitrated a dispute involving member and nonmember loansharks who all made uncollectable loans to the same person. Such an event, especially when consistent with other information, can throw considerable light on a question—in this case, the powers of the boss and relationships among loansharks. The justification for the use of such events is that they are based on data sources that cover a decade and are not arbitrarily selected anecdotes.

CITATIONS

CITATIONS FOR INTRODUCTION

1. Francis A. J. Ianni, *A Family Business: Kinship and Social Control in Organized Crime* (New York: Russell Sage Foundation, 1972); John M. Seidl, " 'Upon the Hip'—A Study of the Criminal Loanshark Industry" (Ph.D. diss., Harvard University, 1968).

2. See the Commission's *Task Force Report: Organized Crime* (Washington, D.C.: 1967), p. 6.

3. See Jess Marcum and Henry Rowen, "How Many Games in Town?—The Pros and Cons of Legalized Gambling," *The Public Interest*, 36 (Summer, 1974), pp. 25–52, for reasonable estimates on the volume of gambling, both legal and illegal, in the U.S.

4. Cressey, *Theft of the Nation: The Structure and Operations of Organized Crime in America* (New York: Harper & Row, 1969); Salerno and John S. Tompkins, *The Crime Confederation: Cosa Nostra and Allied Operations in Organized Crime* (Garden City, N.Y.: Doubleday, 1969).

5. Seidl, " '*Upon the Hip*' "; Gasper, "Organized Crime: An Economic Analysis" (Ph.D. diss., Duke University, 1969).

6. Reinhard Bendix, *Max Weber: An Intellectual Portrait* (Garden City, N.Y.: Doubleday, 1962), p. 418.

CITATIONS FOR CHAPTER I

1. Estes Kefauver, *Crime in America* (Garden City, N.Y.: Doubleday, 1951); U.S. Senate Special Committee to Investigate Organized Crime in Interstate Commerce (Kefauver Committee), *Hearings*, 19 parts in 9 vols., and *Reports*, 4 parts in 1 vol. (Washington, D.C.: U.S. Government Printing Office, 1950–1951).

2. "The Hick Cops Bust Up Joe's Nice Barbecue," *Life* 43:24 (December 9, 1957), pp. 57–59.

3. Bell, "Crime as An American Way of Life," in *The End of Ideology*, rev. ed. (New York: Collier, 1961), pp. 129, 139.

4. U.S. Congress, Senate. Hearings Before the Permanent Subcommittee on Investigations of the Committee on Government Operations, *Organized Crime and Illicit Traffic in Narcotics*. Five parts, 88th Congress (Washington, D.C.: 1963–1964).

5. *Combating Organized Crime: A Report of the 1965 Oyster Bay, New York, Conferences on Combating Organized Crime* (Albany, New York: Office of the Counsel to the Governor, Executive Chamber, State Capitol, 1966), p. 19.

6. President's Commission on Law Enforcement and Administration of Justice, *Task Force Report: Organized Crime*, pp. 1, 6.

7. See Ed Reid, *The Grim Reapers: The Anatomy of Organized Crime in America* (Chicago: Henry Regnery, 1969); Cressey, *Theft of the Nation*; and Salerno and Tompkins, *Crime Confederation*, pp. 274–333.

8. Cressey, *Theft of the Nation*, pp. 109–111.

9. Salerno and Tompkins, *Crime Confederation*, p. 89.

10. Hawkins, "God and the Mafia," *Public Interest*, 14 (Winter, 1969), p. 30.

11. Schelling, "Economic Analysis and Organized Crime," app. D of President's Commission on Law Enforcement and Administration of Justice, *Task Force Report: Organized Crime* (Washington, D.C.: U.S. Government Printing Office, 1967), p. 115.

12. Hawkins, "God and the Mafia," p. 34.

13. Ianni, *A Family Business*, p. 33.

14. *Ibid.*, p. 168, 173.

15. Federal District Court, Newark, New Jersey, 1969: the de Cavalcante Transcripts (1962–1965), vol. III, pp. B47–48. Portions of the transcripts, with commentary, have been published in Henry A. Zeiger, *Sam the Plumber: One Year in the Life of a Cosa Nostra Boss* (New York: New American Library, 1970).

16. De Cavalcante Transcripts, vol. V, p. D182.

17. *Ibid.*, vol. II, pp. A39–41.

18. *Ibid.*, vol. III, p. B17.

19. *Ibid.*, vol. III, pp. B86–99.

20. *Ibid.*, vol. IV, pp. C28–29.

21. *Ibid.*, vol. IV, pp. C254, C257–58.

22. *Ibid.*, vol. V, pp. D23–24.

23. *Ibid.*, vol. V, pp. D174–75.

24. *Ibid.*, vol. VII, pp. F241–43.

25. *Ibid.*, vol. VIII, pp. K17–20.

26. *Ibid.*, vol. VIII, pp. K27–28.

27. *Ibid.*, vol. VIII, p. K49.

28. *Ibid.*, vol. VIII, pp. K98–99.

29. Murray Kempton, "Cosa Nostra—That's Italian for 'Our Headache,'" *Playboy*, December, 1970.

CITATIONS FOR CHAPTER II

1. Cressey, *Theft of the Nation*, p. 114.

2. President's Commission on Law Enforcement and Administration of Justice, *The Challenge of Crime in a Free Society* (Washington, D.C., 1967), p. 1.

3. Ianni, *A Family Business*, p. 153.

4. Cressey, *Theft of the Nation*, pp. 126−127, 165−166. See also Donald R. Cressey, "The Functions and Structure of Criminal Syndicates," app. A of President's Commission on Law Enforcement and Administration of Justice, *Task Force Report: Organized Crime*, pp. 54, 58.

5. Cressey, *Theft of the Nation*, p. 82.

6. U.S. Bureau of the Census. *Census of Population and Housing: 1970 Census Tracts, Final Report* (Washington, D.C., 1972).

7. Data from Kansas City Crime Commission, *Spotlight on Organized Crime in the Kansas City Area* (Kansas City, Missouri, April, 1970).

8. Paul H. Rubin, "The Economic Theory of the Criminal Firm," in Simon Rottenberg, ed., *The Economics of Crime and Punishment* (Washington, D.C.: American Enterprise Institute for Public Policy Research, 1973), pp. 155−166.

9. Cressey, *Theft of the Nation*, and Schelling, "Economic Analysis and Organized Crime," pp. 114−126.

10. See, e.g., the writings of Max Weber, who developed a typology of three types of domination: legal, traditional, and charismatic. A useful overview of Weber's work is provided by Reinhard Bendix in *Max Weber: An Intellectual Portrait*.

11. A study of organized crime in Reading, Pennsylvania, by John Gardiner, found control in the hands of non-Italians. Established in the 1940s, this empire was destroyed in the early 1950s. The individual at the head of the operation reestablished an organized criminal operation in Reading in 1955, but the group did not have continuity; this enterprise was destroyed in the early 1960s. It had drawn upon services of Italian organized criminal groups for expertise (and possibly capital) in gambling operations and for the use of violence to eliminate competition, but it was not controlled by members of these groups. The cyclical feature of organized criminal activity in this city is attributed by Gardiner to the citizens' desire for an "open city," where gambling and vice are available, and their aversion to racketeering and official corruption. Periodically a reform mayor has been elected and has succeeded in eliminating organized criminal activity and official corruption, but no mayor has been able to succeed himself in office. See John A. Gardiner, *The Politics of Corruption: Organized Crime in an American City* (New York: Russell Sage Foundation, 1970).

12. Ianni, *A Family Business*, pp. 165−166, 193.

13. Furstenberg notes that the Italian organized criminal group in New England was inhibited in Boston by three strong Irish criminal organizations who controlled gambling and loansharking. In 1962 violence broke out between

the Irish groups. They were sufficiently depleted and weakened to permit the Italian group to move in and terrorize the Irish competition. See Mark H. Furstenberg, "Violence and Organized Crime," app. 18 to *Crimes of Violence Vol. 13—A Staff Report Submitted to the National Commission on the Causes and Prevention of Violence*, Donald J. Mulvihill and Melvin M. Tumin, codirectors (Washington, D.C.: U.S. Government Printing Office, 1969). A comparison of the internal organizational structure, methods of control, and basis on which the Irish groups established and legitimated quasi-governments, if they did so, would be helpful in identifying the importance of the development of quasi-governments in organized criminal groups; different methods of legitimating such governments; and the significance of the Italian organized criminal group's reliance on kinship.

14. Bell, "Crime as an American Way of Life," pp. 129, 147.

15. See, e.g., Cressey, *Theft of the Nation*; Reid, *The Grim Reapers*; and Furstenberg, "Violence and Organized Crime."

16. Cressey, *Theft of the Nation*, p. 152.

CITATIONS FOR CHAPTER III

1. Cressey, *Theft of the Nation*, p. 134.

2. A public document (which cannot be referenced because to do so would identify the city) notes that from records and raid data seized in the mid and late 1960s, four raided numbers banks not operated by members of the group did an annual volume of business of over $22 million, or $425,000 per week. The document offers no comparable information on member-operated firms.

3. Cressey (*Theft of the Nation*, p. 136) notes that numbers writers (those who take bets from the customer) may receive up to 25 percent of the amount bet. Controllers, who collect the bets from the writers, and office expenses may absorb another 10 percent. Payouts would average under 60 percent, possibly as low as 55 percent. About 10 percent would remain for protection and profit.

4. Thomas C. Schelling, "What Is the Business of Organized Crime?" *The American Scholar*, 40:4 (Autumn, 1971), pp. 643–652.

5. Morris Ploscowe, ed., *Organized Crime and Law Enforcement: The Reports, Research Studies, and Model Statutes and Commentaries Prepared for the American Bar Association Commission on Organized Crime*, 2 vols. (New York: Grosby, 1952), I, 92.

6. Peter Maas, *The Valachi Papers* (New York: G. P. Putnam's Sons, 1968), p. 134n.

7. Paul H. Rubin, "Economic Theory of the Criminal Firm."

8. Schelling, "What Is the Business of Organized Crime?" p. 651.

9. Oswald Jacoby, *Oswald Jacoby on Gambling* (New York: Hart, 1963).

10. Cressey, *Theft of the Nation*, p. 136.

11. See, for example, Cressey, *Theft of the Nation*; Salerno and Tompkins, *Crime Confederation*; and Ianni, *A Family Business*.

CITATIONS FOR CHAPTER IV

1. Seidl, " 'Upon the Hip.' "

2. U.S. Bureau of the Census. *Statistical Abstract of the United States: 1972*, 93rd ed. (Washington, D.C.: 1972).

3. Seidl, " 'Upon the Hip,' " pp. 87−94.

4. Cressey, *Theft of the Nation*, p. 81; Ianni, *A Family Business*, p. 99.

5. A public document concerning organized crime in this city states that thousands of people are employed in the industry. This contradicts the information available to me, but that information is incomplete. The thousands noted in the public document may include borrowers who refer friends and acquaintances to their loanshark.

CITATIONS FOR CHAPTER V

1. See, for example, Peter D. Andreoli, "Organized Crime Enterprises—Legal," in S. A. Yefsky, ed., *Law Enforcement Science and Technology* (London: Thompson Book Company, Academic Press, 1967), pp. 21−27; Salerno and Tompkins, *Crime Confederation*; and other titles in notes to this chap.

2. Ianni, *A Family Business*.

3. *Task Force Report: Organized Crime*, p. 1.

4. Ianni, *A Family Business*, p. 193.

5. David MacMichael, "The Criminal as Businessman: A Discussion of the Legitimate Business Operations of Organized Crime Figures," mimeographed (Stanford Research Institute, January 31, 1971).

6. Melvin K. Bers, "The Penetration of Legitimate Business by Organized Crime—An Analysis," mimeographed (Law Enforcement Assistance Administration, U.S. Department of Justice, Washington, D.C., April 1970).

7. Bell, "Crime as an American Way of Life," pp. 127−150.

8. "The Strike Force: Organized Law Enforcement v. Organized Crime," *Columbia Journal of Law and Social Problems*, 6:3, pp. 496−523.

9. Data from the *Congressional Record*, August 12, 1969 (Washington, D.C.), pp. S9705−710.

10. For a discussion of the tax fraud charge based on a net worth analysis from the viewpoint of the defendant, see Daniel D. Levenson and David R. Andelman, "How to Prepare an Effective Net Worth Statement to Defend Against a Fraud Charge," *Journal of Taxation*, 30:6 (June 1969).

11. U.S. Bureau of the Budget. *Standard Industrial Classification Manual: 1967* (Washington, D.C.: 1967).

12. This system of classification is used by the Bureau of the Census in collecting data on business establishments in the United States. Two-digit codes refer to major groups—e.g., food stores (SIC code 54). Three-digit codes refer to groups and are breakdowns of major groups (e.g., SIC code 541 is for grocery stores and 546 refers to retail bakeries). A four-digit code refers to an industry and is a further breakdown: SIC codes 5462 and 5463 both refer to bakeries, but 5462 represents those that bake and sell, whereas 5463 represents those that only sell.

13. See Gasper, "Organized Crime," pp. 140–142, for state taxes on cigarettes; this dissertation presents an empirical study of traffic in cigarettes on which state taxes have not been paid.

14. Members of several organized criminal groups have investments in Miami. Cressey notes that Miami is controlled by a New York-Miami partnership. It is not clear whether permission from this partnership is required before a member of another group can operate in the Miami area. Areas without long-established organized criminal groups have, according to Cressey, been designated "open territory" by the Cosa Nostra Commission. These are areas in which anyone can operate, whereas areas controlled by a particular group cannot be entered without permission of the group (Cressey, *Theft of the Nation*, pp. 149–150).

CITATION FOR CHAPTER VI

1. Federal District Court, Newark, New Jersey, 1969. *The de Cavalcante Transcripts* (1962–1965), Vol. XIII, p. G3.

CITATIONS FOR CHAPTER VII

1. See Schelling, "What Is the Business of Organized Crime?" pp. 643–652, for a discussion of the use of violence in extortion, criminal monopolization of an industry, and labor racketeering.

2. Philip P. Hannifin, Chairman of the Nevada Gaming Control Board. Statement made at a training conference on organized crime sponsored by the Law Enforcement Assistance Administration, U.S. Department of Justice, February 20, 1972, San Diego, California.

3. Hank Messick, *Lansky* (New York: Berkley Publishing Company, 1971), p. 250.

4. Cressey, *Theft of the Nation*, p. 99.

5. Bers, "Penetration of Legitimate Business by Organized Crime."

6. Ianni, *A Family Business*, p. 88.

7. *Ibid.*, p. 89.

8. *Ibid.*, p. 94.

CITATIONS FOR CHAPTER VIII

1. Eirik Furubotn and Svetozar Pejovich, "Property Rights and Economic Theory: A Survey of Recent Literature," *Journal of Economic Literature*, 10:4 (December, 1972), pp. 1137–1162.

2. Public Law 87–228, Title 18 U.S. Code, sec. 1952; Public Law 87–216, Title 18 U.S. Code, sec. 1084; and Public Law 87–218, Title 18 U.S. Code, sec. 1953.

3. Public Law 90–351, 90th Congress, H.R. 5037 (June 19, 1968).

4. Public Law 91–452, 91st Congress, S. 30 (October 15, 1970).

5. 390 U.S. 39; 390 U.S. 62; 401 U.S. 715.

6. U.S. Department of the Treasury, Internal Revenue Service. *1971 Annual Report of the Commissioner of Internal Revenue* (Washington, D.C., 1972), p. 94.

7. "The Strike Force," pp. 496–523.

8. U.S. Department of Justice. *1970 Annual Report of the Attorney General of the United States* (Washington, D.C., 1971).

9. U.S. Department of the Treasury, *1971 Annual Report of the Commissioner of Internal Revenue*.

10. Herbert J. Miller, Jr., "A Federal Viewpoint on Combatting Organized Crime," *Annals of the American Academy of Political and Social Science*, 347 (May, 1963), pp. 93–103.

11. U.S. Department of Justice, *1970 Annual Report of the Attorney General of the United States*, pp. 48–50.

12. Timothy D. Schellhardt, "Federal Law-Enforcement Aides Switch Strategy: Attack Mob's Growing Role in Legitimate Fields," *Wall Street Journal*, April 19, 1978, p. 40.

13. See "Bank Secrecy Act Is Upheld by Top Court, Backing Federal Access to Customer Data," *Wall Street Journal*, April 2, 1974, p. 4.

14. As, for example, in Cressey, *Theft of the Nation*.

BIBLIOGRAPHY

BOOKS AND MANUSCRIPTS

Albini, Joseph L. *The American Mafia: Genesis of a Legend*. New York: Appleton-Century-Crofts, 1971.

American Bar Association Special Committee on Crime Prevention and Control. *New Perspectives on Urban Crime*. American Bar Association, 1972.

Baker, Arnold B. "A Critical Evaluation of Resource Allocation Efficiency in the Criminal Justice System of Virginia." Ph.D. dissertation, University of California at Santa Barbara, 1972.

Banfield, Edward. *The Unheavenly City: The Nature and Future of Our Urban Crises*. Boston: Little, Brown, 1970.

Barzini, Luigi. *From Caesar to the Mafia*. New York: Bantam, 1972.

————. *The Italians*. New York: Bantam, 1965.

Beccaria, Cesare Bonesana. *An Essay on Crimes and Punishments*. Stanford, Calif.: Academic Reprints, 1953 (repr. of 1819 ed.).

Bendix, Reinhard. *Max Weber: An Intellectual Portrait*. Garden City, N.Y.: Doubleday, 1962.

Bentham, Jeremy. *An Introduction to the Principles of Morals and Legislation*. New York: Hafnew, 1948.

————. *The Theory of Legislation*. London: Routledge & Kegan Paul, 1931.

Church, Albert Marion, III. "An Econometric Model of Crime in California." Ph.D. dissertation, University of California at Santa Barbara, 1971.

Clinard, Marshall B. *The Black Market: A Study of White Collar Crime*. New York: Rinehart, 1952.

Conley, Bryan Charles. "The Impact of Deterrence, Economic Opportunities and Social Status on Regional Variations in Juvenile Property Crime Rates." Ph.D. dissertation, Claremont Graduate School and University Center, 1972.

Cressey, Donald R. *Theft of the Nation: The Structure and Operations of Organized Crime in America*. New York: Harper & Row, 1969.

Demaris, Ovid. *Captive City: Chicago in Chains*. New York: Lyle Stuart, 1969.

Duster, Troy. *The Legislation of Morality: Law, Drugs, and Moral Judgment*. New York: Free Press, 1970.

Fleisher, Belton M. *The Economics of Delinquency*. Chicago: Quadrangle, 1966.

Gage, Nicholas, *The Mafia Is Not an Equal Opportunity Employer*. New York: McGraw-Hill, 1971.

Gardiner, John A. *The Politics of Corruption: Organized Crime in an American City*. New York: Russell Sage Foundation, 1970.

Gartner, Michael, ed. *Crime and Business: What You Should Know About the Infiltration of Crime into Business—and of Business into Crime*. Princeton, N.J.: Dow Jones Books, 1971. A collection of articles first appearing in *The Wall Street Journal*, 1968–1971.

Gasper, Louis C. "Organized Crime: An Economic Analysis." Ph.D. dissertation, Duke University, 1969.

Halper, Albert, ed. *The Chicago Crime Book*. New York: Pyramid, 1969.

Heidenheimer, Arnold J., ed. *The Analysis of Political Corruption*. New York: Holt, Rinehart & Winston, 1971.

Hirsch, Phil, ed. *The Mafia*. New York: Pyramid, 1971.

Holahan, John F. "Benefit-Cost Analysis of Programs in the Criminal Justice System." Ph.D. dissertation, Georgetown University, 1971.

Ianni, Francis A. J. *A Family Business: Kinship and Social Control in Organized Crime*. New York: Russell Sage Foundation, 1972.

Jacoby, Oswald. *Oswald Jacoby on Gambling*. New York: Hart, 1963.

Jennings, Dean. *We Only Kill Each Other: The Life and Bad Times of Bugsy Siegel*. Greenwich, Conn.: Fawcett, 1968.

Kaplan, John. *Marijuana: The New Prohibition*. New York: Pocket Books, 1971.

Kaplan, Lawrence J., and Dennis Kessler. *An Economic Analysis of Crime: Selected Readings*. Springfield, Ill.: Charles C. Thomas, 1976.

Kennedy, Robert F. *The Enemy Within*. New York: Popular Library, 1960.

King, Rufus. *Gambling and Organized Crime*. Washington, D.C.: Public Affairs Press, 1969.

Kreig, Margaret. *Black Market Medicine*. New York: Bantam, 1967.

Lasswell, Harold D., and Jeremiah B. McKenna. *The Impact of Organized Crime on an Inner City Community*. New York: Policy Sciences Center, 1971.

Maas, Peter. *The Valachi Papers*. New York: G. P. Putnam's Sons, 1968.

McLennan, Barbara N., ed. *Crime in Urban Society*. New York: Dunellen, 1970.

Merton, Robert K. *Social Theory and Social Structure*. Revised ed. New York: Free Press, 1957.

Messick, Hank. *Lansky*. New York: Berkley Publishing Company, 1971.

Mills, C. W. *The New Men of Power*. New York: Harcourt, Brace, 1948.

Mollenhoff, Clark R. *Strike Force: Organized Crime and the Government*. Englewood Cliffs, N.J.: Prentice-Hall, 1972.

Morris, Norval, and Gordon Hawkins. *The Honest Politician's Guide to Crime Control*. Chicago: University of Chicago Press, 1970.

Norsworthy, J. Randolph. "A Theory of Taxpayer Behavior: Evasion of the Personal Income Tax." Ph.D. dissertation, University of Virginia, 1966.

Ploscowe, Morris, ed. *Organized Crime and Law Enforcement: The Reports, Research Studies, and Model Statutes and Commentaries Prepared for the American Bar Association Commission on Organized Crime*. 2 vols. New York: Grosby, 1952.

Reid, Ed. *The Grim Reapers: The Anatomy of Organized Crime in America*. Chicago: Henry Regnery, 1969.

Reid, Ed, and Ovid Demaris. *The Green Felt Jungle*. New York: Pocket Books, 1964.

Reynolds, Morgan O. "Crimes for Profit: Economics of Theft." Ph.D. dissertation, University of Wisconsin, 1971.

Ribich, Thomas I. *Education and Poverty*. Washington, D.C.: Brookings Institution, 1968.

Rottenberg, Simon, ed. *The Economics of Crime and Punishment*. Washington, D.C.: American Enterprise Institute for Public Policy Research, 1973.

Rubner, Alex. *The Economics of Gambling*. London: Macmillan, 1966.

Salerno, Ralph, and John S. Tompkins. *The Crime Confederation: Cosa Nostra and Allied Operations in Organized Crime*. Garden City, N.Y.: Doubleday, 1969.

Schur, Edwin M. *Crimes Without Victims: Deviant Behavior and Public Policy*. Englewood Cliffs, N.J.: Prentice-Hall, 1965.

———. *Our Criminal Society: The Social and Legal Sources of Crime in America*. Englewood Cliffs, N.J.: Prentice-Hall, 1969.

Seidl, John M. " 'Upon the Hip'—A Study of the Criminal Loanshark Industry." Ph.D. dissertation, Harvard University, 1968.

Shoup, Carl S. *Public Finance*. Chicago: Aldine, 1969.

Sjoquist, David Laurence. "Property Crime as an Economic Phenomenon." Ph.D. dissertation, University of Minnesota, 1971.

Smigel, Arleen. "Crime and Punishment: An Economic Analysis." Master's thesis, Columbia University, 1965.

Talese, Gay. *Honor Thy Father*. Greenwich, Conn.: Fawcett, 1971.

Tyler, Gus, ed. *Organized Crime in America: A Book of Readings*. Ann Arbor: University of Michigan Press, 1962.

Vold, George B. *Theoretical Criminology*. New York: Oxford University Press, 1958.

Yefsky, S. A., ed. *Law Enforcement Science and Technology: Proceedings of First National Symposium on Law Enforcement Science and Technology*. London: Thompson Book Company, Academic Press, 1967.

Zeiger, Henry A. *Sam the Plumber: One Year in the Life of a Cosa Nostra Boss*. New York: New American Library, 1970.

ARTICLES

Anderson, Annelise. "Organized Crime: The Need for Research," *University of Florida Law Review,* 24:1 (Fall, 1971), pp. 42–57.

Andreoli, Peter D. "Organized Crime Enterprises—Legal." In S. A. Yefsky, ed., *Law Enforcement Science and Technology.* London: Thompson Book Company, Academic Press, 1967, pp. 21–27.

Becker, Gary S. "Crime and Punishment: An Economic Approach," *Journal of Political Economy,* 26:2 (Mar./Apr., 1968), pp. 169–217.

Bell, Daniel. "Crime as an American Way of Life." In *The End of Ideology.* Revised ed. New York: Collier, 1961, pp. 127–150.

———. "The Racket-Ridden Longshoremen: The Web of Economics and Politics." In *The End of Ideology.* Revised ed. New York: Collier, 1961, pp. 175–209.

Blakey, G. Robert. "Organized Crime and Corruption Practices." In S. A. Yefsky, ed., *Law Enforcement Science and Technology.* London: Thompson Book Company, Academic Press, 1967, pp. 15–20.

Blakey, G. Robert. "Organized Crime in the United States," *Current History,* 52:310 (June, 1967), pp. 327–333, 364–365.

Blitz, Rudolph C., and Millard F. Long. "The Economics of Usury Regulation," *Journal of Political Economy,* 73:6 (Dec., 1965), pp. 608–619.

Buchanan, James M. "A Defense of Organized Crime?" In Simon Rottenberg, ed., *The Economics of Crime and Punishment.* Washington, D.C.: American Enterprise Institute for Public Policy Research, 1973, pp. 119–132.

Coase, R. H. "The Problem of Social Cost," *Journal of Law and Economics,* 3 (1960), pp. 1–44.

Cook, Fred J. "Gambling, Inc.: Treasure Chest of the Underworld," *The Nation,* 191:13 (Oct. 22, 1960), pp. 257–316.

Cressey, Donald R. "The Functions and Structure of Criminal Syndicates." Appendix A of President's Commission on Law Enforcement and Administration of Justice, *Task Force Report: Organized Crime.* Washington, D.C.: U.S. Government Printing Office, 1967, pp. 26–60.

———. "Methodological Problems in the Study of Organized Crime as a Social Problem," *Annals of the American Academy of Political and Social Science,* 347 (Nov., 1967), pp. 101–112.

Dosser, Douglas S. "Notes on Carl S. Shoup's Standards for Distributing a Free Governmental Service: Crime Prevention," *Public Finance,* 19:4 (Dec., 1964), pp. 393–461.

Downs, Anthony. "Round Table on Allocation of Resources in Law Enforcement," *American Economic Review,* 59:2 (May, 1969), pp. 504–505.

Duffy, William J. "Organized Crime—Illegal Activities." In S. A. Yefsky, ed., *Law Enforcement Science and Technology.* London: Thompson Book Company, Academic Press, 1967, pp. 29–32.

Ehrlich, Isaac. "The Time Trend of Crime in the United States." In *Fifty-First Annual Report of the National Bureau of Economic Research*. New York: NBER, Sept., 1971, pp. 106–107.

Erickson, Edward. "The Social Cost of the Discovery and Suppression of the Clandestine Distribution of Heroin," *Journal of Political Economy*, 77 (July/Aug., 1969).

Evans, Robert, Jr. "The Labor Market and Parole Success," *Journal of Human Resources*, 3:2 (Summer, 1968), pp. 201–212.

Fernandez, Raul A. "The Clandestine Distribution of Heroin, Its Discovery and Suppression: A Comment," *Journal of Political Economy*, 77 (July/Aug., 1969).

Firey, Walter. "Limits to Economy in Crime and Punishment," *Social Science Quarterly*, 50:1 (June, 1969) pp. 72–77.

Fleisher, Belton M. "The Effect of Income on Delinquency," *American Economic Review*, 56:1 (Mar., 1966), pp. 118–137.

———. "The Effect of Income on Delinquency: Reply," *American Economic Review*, 60:1 (Mar., 1970), p. 257.

———. "The Effect of Unemployment on Juvenile Delinquency," *Journal of Political Economy*, 71:1 (Dec., 1963), pp. 543–555.

Friedman, Milton, and Leonard J. Savage. "The Utility Analysis of Choices Involving Risk," *Journal of Political Economy*, 56 (1948).

Furstenberg, Mark H. "Violence and Organized Crime." Appendix 18 to *Crimes of Violence Vol. 13—A Staff Report Submitted to the National Commission on the Causes and Prevention of Violence*, Donald J. Mulvihill and Melvin M. Tumin, codirectors. Washington, D.C.: U.S. Government Printing Office, 1969.

Furubotn, Eirik, and Svetozar Pejovich. "Property Rights and Economic Theory: A Survey of Recent Literature," *Journal of Economic Literature*, 10:4 (Dec., 1972), pp. 1137–1162.

Gould, John P. "On the Economics of Going to Court." Center for Mathematic Studies in Business and Economics, University of Chicago, report 6836 (Sept., 1968).

Gutmann, Peter M. "The Subterranean Economy," *Financial Analysts Journal* (Nov./Dec., 1977), pp. 26–27, 34.

Harris, John R. "On the Economics of Law and Order," *Journal of Political Economy*, 78:1 (Jan./Feb., 1970), pp. 165–174.

Hatry, Harry P. "Measuring the Effectiveness of Nondefense Public Programs," *Operations Research*, 18:5 (Sept./Oct., 1970), pp. 772–784.

Hawkins, Gordon. "God and the Mafia," The *Public Interest*, 14 (Winter, 1969), pp. 24–51.

"The Hick Cops Bust Up Joe's Nice Barbecue," *Life*, 43:24 (December 9, 1957), pp. 57–59.

Hoffman, Richard B. "Round Table on Allocation of Resources in Law Enforcement," *American Economic Review*, 59:2 (May, 1969), pp. 510–512.

Ianni, Francis A. J. "Formal and Social Organization in an Organized Crime 'Family': A Case Study," *University of Florida Law Review*, 24:1 (Fall, 1971), pp. 31–41.

———. "The Mafia and the Web of Kinship," *The Public Interest*, 22 (Winter, 1971), pp. 78–110.

Johnson, Earl, Jr. "Organized Crime: Challenge to the American Legal System," *Journal of Criminal Law, Criminology, and Police Science*, 53:4 (Dec., 1962), pp. 399–425; 54:1 (Mar., 1963), pp. 1–29; 54:2 (June, 1963), pp. 127–145.

Kaplan, Lawrence J., and Salvatore Matteis. "The Economics of Loansharking," *American Journal of Economics and Sociology*, 27 (July, 1968), pp. 239–252.

Kelton, Harold W., Jr., and Charles M. Unkovic. "Characteristics of Organized Criminal Groups," *Canadian Journal of Corrections*, 13:1 (Jan., 1971), pp. 68–78.

Kempton, Murray. "Cosa Nostra—That's Italian for 'Our Headache,' " *Playboy*, Dec., 1970.

———. "Crime Does Not Pay," *The New York Review of Books*, 13:4 (Sept., 11, 1969), pp. 5–9.

Kessel, Reuben. "Economic Effects of Public Regulation of Milk Markets," *Journal of Law and Economics*, 10 (1967), pp. 51–77.

Landes, William M. "An Economic Analysis of the Courts," *Journal of Law and Economics*, 14:1 (Apr., 1971), pp. 61–108.

———. "Law and Economics." In *Fifty-First Annual Report of the National Bureau of Economic Research*, New York: NBER, Sept., 1971, pp. 2–8.

Lee, Dwight R. "Utility Analysis and Repetitive Gambling," *The American Economist*, 14:2 (Fall, 1969), pp. 87–91.

Lefkowitz, Louis J. "New York: Criminal Infiltration of the Securities Industry," *Annals of the American Academy of Political and Social Science*, 347 (May, 1963), pp. 51–57.

Levenson, Daniel D., and David R. Andelman. "How to Prepare an Effective Net Worth Statement to Defend Against a Fraud Charge," *Journal of Taxation*, 30:6 (June, 1969).

Lippmann, Walter. "The Underworld—A Stultified Conscience," *Forum*, 85:2 (Feb., 1931), pp. 65–69.

"Loan-Sharking: The Untouched Domain of Organized Crime," *Columbia Journal of Law and Social Problems*, 5:91 (1969), pp. 91–136.

MacMichael, David. "The Criminal as Businessman: A Discussion of the Legitimate Business Operations of Organized Crime Figures." Mimeographed. Stanford Research Institute, Jan. 31, 1971.

Marcum, Jess, and Henry Rowen. "How Many Games in Town?—The Pros and Cons of Legalized Gambling," *The Public Interest*, 36 (Summer, 1974), pp. 25–52.

Miller, Herbert J., Jr. "A Federal Viewpoint on Combatting Organized Crime," *Annals of the American Academy of Political and Social Science*, 347 (May, 1963), pp. 93–103.

Mishan, E. F. "A Note on the Costs of Tariffs, Monopolies and Thefts," *Western Economic Journal*, 7 (Sept., 1969), pp. 230–233.

Nutter, Warren G. "The Case Theorem on Social Cost: A Footnote," *Journal of Law and Economics*, 11 (1968), pp. 503–507.

Peterson, Virgil W. "Chicago: Shades of Capone," *Annals of the American Academy of Political and Social Science*, 347 (May, 1963), pp. 30–39.

Pileggi, Nicholas. "The Lying, Thieving, Murdering, Upper-Middle-Class, Respectable Crook," *Esquire* (Jan., 1966), pp. 50ff.

Preble, Edward, and John J. Casey, Jr. "Taking Care of Business—The Heroin User's Life on the Street," *International Journal of the Addictions*, 4:1 (Mar., 1969), pp. 1–24.

Rottenberg, Simon. "The Clandestine Distribution of Heroin, Its Discovery and Suppression," *Journal of Political Economy*, 76:1 (Jan./Feb., 1968), pp. 78–90.

———. "The Social Cost of Crime and Crime Prevention." In Barbara N. McLennan, ed., *Crime in Urban Society*. New York: Dunellen, 1970.

Rubin, Paul H. "The Economic Theory of the Criminal Firm." In Simon Rottenberg, ed., *The Economics of Crime and Punishment*. Washington, D.C.: American Enterprise Institute for Public Policy Research, 1973, pp. 155–166.

Sanders, P. H., ed. "Combating the Loan Shark," *Law and Contemporary Problems*, 3:1 (Winter, 1941).

Schellhardt, Timothy D. "Federal Law-Enforcement Aides Switch Strategy: Attack Mob's Growing Role in Legitimate Fields," *Wall Street Journal*, April 19, 1978, p. 40.

Schelling, Thomas C. "Economic Analysis and Organized Crime," Appendix D of President's Commission on Law Enforcement and Administration of Justice, *Task Force Report: Organized Crime*. Washington, D.C.: U.S. Government Printing Office, 1967, pp. 114–126.

———. "What Is the Business of Organized Crime?" *American Scholar*, 40:4 (Autumn, 1971), pp. 643–652.

Shoup, Carl S. "Standards for Distributing a Free Governmental Service: Crime Prevention," *Public Finance*, 19:4 (Dec., 1964), pp. 383–392.

Stigler, George. "Economic Effects of Antitrust Laws," *Journal of Law and Economics*, 9 (1966), pp. 225–258.

———. "The Optimum Enforcement of Laws," *Journal of Political Economy*, 78:3 (May/June, 1970), pp. 526–536.

———. "Private Vice and Public Virtue," *Journal of Law and Economics*, 4 (1961).

"The Strike Force: Organized Law Enforcement v. Organized Crime," *Columbia Journal of Law and Social Problems*, 6:3, pp. 496–523.

Sullivan, Richard F. "Economics of Crime: An Introduction to the Literature," *Crime and Delinquency*, 19:138 (April, 1973).

Taft, Philip. "Corruption and Racketeering in the Labor Movement." New York State School of Industrial and Labor Relations, Cornell University, bulletin 38 (Feb., 1958), pp. 32–33.

Thurow, Lester C., and Carl Rappaport. "Law Enforcement and Cost-Benefit Analysis," *Public Finance*, 24:1 (1969), pp. 48–63.

Tittle, Charles R. "Punishment and Deterrence of Deviance." In Simon Rottenberg, ed., *The Economics of Crime and Punishment*. Washington, D.C.: American Enterprise Institute for Public Policy Research, 1973, pp. 85–102.

Tullock, Gordon. "An Economic Approach to Crime," *Social Science Quarterly*, 50:1 (June, 1969), pp. 59–71.

———. "The Welfare Costs of Tariffs, Monopolies and Theft," *Western Economic Journal*, 5 (June, 1967), pp. 224–232.

Tyler, Gus. "The Roots of Organized Crime," *Crime and Delinquency*, 8:4 (Oct., 1962), pp. 325–338.

Weicher, John C. "The Effect of Income on Delinquency: A Comment," *American Economic Review*, 60:4 (Mar., 1970), pp. 249–256.

Woetzel, Robert K. "An Overview of Organized Crime: Mores versus Morality," *Annals of the American Academy of Political and Social Science*, 347 (May, 1963), pp. 1–11.

PUBLIC DOCUMENTS

Bers, Melvin K. "The Penetration of Legitimate Business by Organized Crime— An Analysis." Mimeographed. Law Enforcement Assistance Administration, U.S. Department of Justice, Washington, D.C., April 1970.

Chicago Crime Commission. *A Report on Chicago Crime*. Chicago: 1960, 1967, 1968 (annual).

Combating Organized Crime: A Report of the 1965 Oyster Bay, New York, Conferences on Combating Organized Crime. Albany, New York: Office of the Counsel to the Governor, Executive Chamber, State Capitol, 1966.

Commission on the Review of the National Policy toward Gambling. *Gambling in America: Final Report*. Washington, D.C.: U.S. Government Printing Office, 1976.

Congressional Record, 91st Cong., 1st sess. Washington D.C., Aug. 12, 1969, pp. S9705–710.

Edelhertz, Herbert. *The Nature, Impact and Prosecution of White-Collar Crime*. Law Enforcement Assistance Administration, U.S. Department of Justice, Washington, D.C., 1970.

Federal District Court, Newark, New Jersey, 1969. Transcripts of electronic surveillance of Sam de Cavalcante, 1962–1965 (known as the de Cavalcante Transcripts).

Ianni, Francis A. J. "Ethnic Succession and Network Formation in Organized Crime." Final report, grant award no. NI-71-076-G. Law Enforcement Assistance Administration, U.S. Department of Justice, Washington, D.C., n.d. [1971?].

National Commission on the Causes and Prevention of Violence, Donald J. Mulvihill and Melvin M. Tumin, codirectors. *Crimes of Violence Vol. 13—A Staff Report.* Washington, D.C., 1969.

[New York City] Commission to Investigate Alleged Police Corruption. *Commission Report.* New York, Dec. 26, 1972.

New York State Temporary Commission of Investigation. *An Investigation of Law Enforcement in Buffalo.* New York, 1961.

———. *The Loan Shark Racket.* New York, 1965.

———. *Syndicated Gambling in New York State.* New York, 1961.

President's Commission on Law Enforcement and Administration of Justice. *The Challenge of Crime in a Free Society.* Washington, D.C., 1967.

———. *Task Force Report: Assessment of Crime.* Washington, D.C., 1967.

———. *Task Force Report: Organized Crime.* Washington, D.C., 1967.

Public Law 87–216, Title 18 U.S. Code, sec. 1084.

Public Law 87–218, Title 18 U.S. Code, sec. 1953.

Public Law 87–228, Title 18 U.S. Code, sec. 1952.

Public Law 90–321, May 29, 1968. Title 18 USCA. (supp. 1969). Title II of the Consumer Credit Protection Act of 1968, "Extortionate Credit Transactions."

Public Law 90–351. 90th Congress, H.R. 5037. June 19, 1968. Omnibus Crime Control and Safe Streets Act of 1968.

Public Law 91–452. 91st Congress, S. 30. Oct. 15, 1970. Organized Crime Control Act of 1970.

Public Law 91–644. 91st Congress, H.R. 17825. Jan. 2, 1971. Omnibus Crime Control and Safe Streets Act Amendments.

Roselius, Ted, and Douglas Benton. "Marketing Theory and the Fencing of Stolen Goods" (Apr., 1971). Report submitted to the Law Enforcement Assistance Administration, U.S. Department of Justice, Washington, D.C.

Smith, Gerald W., and Wen Li. "A Survey of Gambling in the United States." Report submitted to the Law Enforcement Assistance Administration, U.S. Department of Justice, Washington, D.C., 1971.

U.S. Bureau of the Budget. *Standard Industrial Classification Manual: 1967.* Washington, D.C., 1967.

U.S. Bureau of the Census. *Census of Population and Housing: 1970 Census Tracts.* Final Report. Washington, D.C., 1972.

────. *Statistical Abstract of the United States: 1972,* 93rd ed., Washington, D.C., 1972.

U.S. Congress. House. Hearings before a Subcommittee of the Committee on Government Operations. *Federal Effort Against Organized Crime.* 3 pts. and report. 90th Congress. Washington, D.C., 1967–1968.

────. Hearings Before a Subcommittee of the Committee on Government Operations. *Federal Effort against Organized Crime: Role of the Private Sector.* 91st Congress, 2nd sess. Washington, D.C., 1970.

U.S. Congress. Senate. Hearings Before the Permanent Subcommittee on Investigations of the Committee on Government Operations. *Organized Crime and Illicit Traffic in Narcotics.* 5 pts. 88th Congress. Washington, D.C., 1963–1964.

────. Hearings Before a Subcommittee on Criminal Laws and Procedures of the Committee on the Judiciary. *Controlling Crime through More Effective Law Enforcement.* 90th Congress, 1st sess. Washington, D.C., 1967.

────. Report of the Committee on Government Operations Made by Its Permanent Subcommittee on Investigations. *Organized Crime and Illicit Traffic in Narcotics.* 89th Congress, 1st sess. Washington, D.C., 1965.

U.S. Congress. Senate Special Committee to Investigate Organized Crime in Interstate Commerce (Kefauver Committee). *Hearings,* 19 parts in 9 vols.; and *Reports,* 4 parts in 1 vol. (Washington, D.C.: U.S. Government Printing Office, 1950–1951).

U.S. Department of Justice. *1970 Annual Report of the Attorney General of the United States.* Washington, D.C., 1971.

U.S. Department of the Treasury, Internal Revenue Service. *1971 Annual Report of the Commissioner of Internal Revenue.* Washington, D.C., 1972.

────. *Digest of Wagering Operations.* Document no. 5466 (1–63). Washington, D.C., n.d.

INDEX

Advisory Task Force on Organized
Crime, 138n
Apalachin (New York) meeting, 9,
10, 128
Armed robberies, 27
Arson, 86, 123, 138

Bandy, Joe. *See* Biondo, Joseph
Bankruptcy fraud, 122, 123
Banks, 98
Bank Secrecy Act of 1970, 141
Barbera, Joseph, 128
Bars, 82, 85, 86–87, 91, 95, 109,
110, 128, 130
Bayonne, Joe. *See* Zicarelli, Joseph
Arthur
Bell, Daniel, 12, 76; quoted, 9, 48
Benguerra family: activities of, 1–2,
34, 37–38, 39, 52–58, 59–60,
62, 64–73 passim, 77–115, 117,
120–128 passim, 133, 134, 135,
136, 140–146 passim (*see also*
Legitimate activities of organized
criminal groups; Loansharking;
Numbers gambling); age and
income relationships in, 106–
107, 114, 126; age distribution
of, 41, 42 (fig.), 43, 44; associates
of, 39–41, 43–44, 65, 73, 75,
88, 90, 103, 109, 110; background of, 1; behavior standards
in, 45; Calabrians in, 34, 35, 48;
composition of, 1, 3, 34–35,
39–40, 41, 43, 73, 126; data
sources used for study of, 147–
154; economic structure of, 34,

35, 36, 45, 49, 77–78, 103,
105–108, 113, 126–128; income-wealth class of individuals
in, 105–108, 113, 126, 127 (table); internal services of, 37–38,
45, 57–58, 60, 79, 103, 111,
112; government investigation
of, 78, 114; loans within, 38, 57;
location of, 148; organization
structure of, 2, 34–37; as pseudonym, 1n; quasi-governmental
functions of, 34, 45, 49, 77, 136;
recruitment in, 43, 48; research
methods used in study of, 147–
154; Sicilians in, 34, 35, 48; size
of, 39, 43, 148; as threat to competitors or community, 140; tax
evasion by (*see* Tax evasion); use
of violence by, 45–46, 66, 71,
77, 103, 117–118
Berman, Otto (Abbadabba), 56
Bers, Melvin K., 76, 128–129, 130,
135
Biondo, Joseph (alias Joe Bandy), 30,
31
Blacks in organized crime, 39, 47;
numbers gambling, 62
Bonanno, Joe, role in Cosa Nostra,
17–30 passim, 33
Bonanno, Salvatore Vincent (Bill),
19, 22
Bonanno family, 16, 19, 28
Bookmaking, 39, 59–60, 63, 110
Bootlegging, 1, 138
Borgata. See Family
Boss, 15, 35; functions of, 2, 36,
37–38, 97

ABOUT THE AUTHOR

Annelise Anderson was the first project manager of organized crime research at the Law Enforcement Assistance Administration (LEAA) in the U.S. Department of Justice in Washington, D.C. In 1972 she was a member of the Advisory Task Force on Organized Crime of the National Commission on Criminal Justice Standards and Goals, and in 1975 served on a five-person LEAA team that evaluated the Office of the Special Prosecutor of New York State. She is the author of several articles on organized crime and public policy and was a consultant to the Commission on the Review of the National Policy Toward Gambling.

Anderson received her A.B. degree from Wellesley College in 1960, an M.A. from Columbia University in 1965, and a Ph.D. in business administration from the Graduate School of Business of Columbia University in 1974. In 1968 she was a researcher and speechwriter in Richard Nixon's presidential campaign. She is currently an assistant professor of Business Administration at California State University, Hayward, where she teaches economics and corporation finance in both the undergraduate and graduate programs. Dr. Anderson is also a research fellow at The Hoover Institution, Stanford University.